W9-BXH-033

What Can I Do Now?

Sports

Second Edition

Books in the
What Can I Do Now? Series

Art
Computers
Engineering, Second Edition
Fashion
Health Care
Music
Nursing, Second Edition
Radio and Television, Second Edition
Safety and Security, Second Edition
Sports, Second Edition

What Can I Do Now?

Sports

Second Edition

Ferguson

An imprint of Infobase Publishing

What Can I Do Now? Sports, Second Edition

Ferguson
An imprint of Infobase Publishing
132 West 31st Street
New York NY 10001

ISBN-10: 0-8160-6034-7
ISBN-13: 978-0-8160-6034-4

Library of Congress Cataloging-in-Publication Data
What can I do now? Sports. — 2nd ed.
    p. cm.
  Rev. ed. of: Preparing for a career in sports. c1998.
  Includes bibliographical references and index.
  ISBN 0-8160-6034-7 (hc : alk. paper)
  1. Sports—Vocational guidance—United States—Juvenile literature.
I. J.G. Ferguson Publishing Company. II. Preparing for a career in sports. III. Title:
Sports.
  GV734.3.W43 2007
  796'.023—dc22   2006031865

Ferguson books are available at special discounts when purchased in bulk quantities for businesses, associations, institutions, or sales promotions. Please call our Special Sales Department in New York at (212) 967-8800 or (800) 322-8755.

You can find Ferguson on the World Wide Web at http://www.fergpubco.com

Text design by Kerry Casey
Cover design by Takeshi Takahashi

Printed in the United States of America

VB Hermitage 10 9 8 7 6 5 4 3 2 1

This book is printed on acid-free paper.

All links and web addresses were checked and verified to be correct at the time of publication. Because of the dynamic nature of the web, some addresses and links may have changed since publication and may no longer be valid.

Contents

Introduction

If you are considering a career in sports—which presumably you are since you're reading this book—you must realize that the better informed you are from the start, the better your chances of having a successful, satisfying career.

There is absolutely no reason to wait until you get out of high school to "get serious" about a career. That doesn't mean you have to make a firm, undying commitment right now. Indeed, one of the biggest fears most people face at some point (sometimes more than once) is choosing the right career. Frankly, many people don't "choose" at all. They take a job because they need one, and all of a sudden 10 years have gone by and they wonder why they're stuck doing something they hate. Don't be one of those people! You have the opportunity right now—while you're still in high school and still relatively unencumbered with major adult responsibilities—to explore, to experience, to try out a work path. Or several paths if you're one of those over-achieving types. Wouldn't you really rather find out sooner than later that you're not cut out to be a professional athlete after all, that you'd actually prefer to be a sports statistician? Or an umpire? Or a sports physician?

There are many ways to explore the sports industry. What we've tried to do in this book is give you an idea of some of your options. Section 1, What Do I Need to Know About the Sports Industry?, will give you an overview of the field—a little history, where it's at today, and promises of the future, as well as a breakdown of its structure (how it's organized) and a glimpse of some of its many career options.

Section 2, Careers, includes 10 chapters, each describing in detail a specific sports specialty: athletic trainer, grounds-manager and groundskeeper, professional athlete, sports broadcaster, sports coach, sports executive, sports physician and surgeon, sports statistician, sportswriter, and umpire and referee. The educational requirements for these specialties range from high school diploma to M.D. These chapters rely heavily on firsthand accounts from real people on the job. They'll tell you what skills you need, what personal qualities you have to have, what the ups and downs of the jobs are. You'll also find out about educational requirements—including specific high school and college classes—advancement possibilities, related jobs, salary ranges, and the future outlook.

In keeping with the secondary theme of this book (the primary theme, for those of you who still don't get it, is You can do something now), Section 3, Do It Yourself, urges you to take charge and start your own programs and activities where none exist—school, community, or the nation. Why not?

The real meat of the book is in Section 4, What Can I Do Right Now? This is where you get busy and *do something*. The chapter "Get Involved" will clue you in on the obvious volunteer and intern positions, the not-so-obvious summer camps and summer college study, and other opportunities.

While the best way to explore sports is to jump right in and start doing it, there are plenty of other ways to get into the sports mind-set. "Surf the Web" offers you a short annotated list of sports-related Web sites where you can explore everything from job listings (start getting an idea of what employers are looking for now) to educational and certification requirements to on-the-job accounts.

"Read a Book" is an annotated bibliography of books (some new, some old) and periodicals. If you're even remotely considering a career in sports, reading a few books and checking out a few magazines is the easiest thing you can do. Don't stop with our list. Ask your librarian to point you to more sports-related materials.

"Ask for Money" is a sampling of sports scholarships. You need to be familiar with these because you're going to need money for school. You have to actively pursue scholarships; no one is going to come up to you in the hall one day and present you with a check because you're such a wonderful student. Applying for scholarships is work. It takes effort. And it must be done right and often a year in advance of when you need the money.

"Look to the Pros" is the final chapter. It's a list of professional organizations that you can turn to for more information about accredited schools, education requirements, career descriptions, salary information, job listings, scholarships, and much more. Once you become a college student, you'll be able to join some of these. Time after time, professionals say that membership and active participation in a professional organization is one of the best ways to network (make valuable contacts) and gain recognition in a particular field.

High school can be a lot of fun. There are dances and football games; maybe you're in the band or play a sport. Or maybe you hate school and are just biding your time until you graduate. Whoever you are, take a minute and try to imagine your life five years from now. Ten years from now. Where will you be? What will you be doing? Whether you realize it or not, how you choose to spend your time now—studying, playing, watching TV, working at a fast-food restaurant, hanging out, whatever—will have an impact on your future. Take a look at how you're spending your time and ask yourself, "Where is this getting me?" If you can't come up with an answer, it's probably "nowhere." The choice is yours. No one is going to take you by the hand and lead you in the "right" direction. It's up to you. It's your life. You can do something about it right now!

SECTION 1

What Do I Need to Know About the Sports Industry?

Imagine that someone asks you, "How would you like a career in sports?" Is your first response to picture LeBron James flying through the air and reply, "Yeah, right. Maybe in my dreams?" If it is, then you're being too hasty. The sports industry offers a huge variety of jobs for people who love sports, even if you don't actually play a sport at all.

Take a look, for example, at the staff of a typical minor league baseball team. On its active roster, the team has 12 pitchers, two catchers, five infielders, and six outfielders—for a total of 25 active players. This might sound like a lot until you see the number of employees in nonplayer positions. Working directly with the players is a manager, a hitting coach, a pitching coach, a trainer, a clubhouse manager, and a person in charge of uniforms and laundry. In the front office, the team employs a general manager, an assistant general manager, an office manager, a group sales manager, a broadcaster for both home and away games, four marketing specialists, and eight full-time souvenir and sales staff members. Three groundskeepers prepare the field before and during each home game, and a crew of five cleans the stadium with power hoses in the early morning hours. Finally, on game days, the team hires up to 60 seasonal employees to work in concessions and as parking lot attendants and ticket takers, plus a dancer and acrobat to perform as a mascot. This makes a total of 118 employees who work for the team in a nonathletic capacity—almost five times the number of athletes! A major-league team carries the same number of players on its roster, but it would employ a much larger nonperformance staff in every category.

This book discusses work as athletes, but it also covers the professional employment possibilities in sports as coaches and trainers, sportswriters and announcers, scouts, agents, and attorneys. Administrative jobs are available in the offices of sports teams, leagues, and associations, or you might prefer to get out on the field as a referee, umpire, or groundskeeper. You can do some of the jobs in this industry right out of high school. Others require special certification, two- or four-year college degrees, or even graduate or professional study.

Perhaps best of all, the sports industry allows you to combine your love of sports with your other interests and skills. Are you mechanically inclined? Maybe you'd like to try servicing race cars as they come screaming into the pit. Is fashion your hobby? You might consider becoming an athletic apparel designer. Do you enjoy kids? Physical education teacher could be the job for you. And we've mentioned only a very few of the job possibilities in the world of sports.

While still in high school, there are many things you can do to prepare yourself for this field. Of course, if you're an athlete and have an eye on making it as a professional, then you must already be working hard toward this goal. But if you aren't an athlete, or if you play a sport but can't foresee making it your career, there are still steps you can take right now to learn about, and even work in, the industry. This book is a good place to start.

GENERAL INFORMATION

The first organized athletic events took place in Greece in 776 B.C., with the advent of the ancient Olympic games. The Olympics featured running races, throwing contests, and other competitive events, with the greatest athletes from the Greek empire competing. The Olympics, even then, were very colorful events that people from nearby countries gathered to watch. The ancient Romans, although initially scornful of sports, also participated, largely as spectators, in athletic events such as chariot races and gladiator battles.

Different cultures and societies developed different sporting pastimes. Bowling, for example, has been around for centuries; a stone ball and nine stone pins were found in the tomb of an ancient Egyptian child. North American Indian tribes played lacrosse with webbed sticks and hard wooden balls centuries ago. Soccer, perhaps the most widely played sport, is believed to have first been played in England in about 200 A.D.

Although the interest in sports diminished during the Middle Ages, sports for entertainment began to reemerge around 1200 A.D. in various European countries. In France, for example, teams played a hockey-like game called la soule. Although la soule was discouraged by authorities because it was thought to be too rough, the sport generated an interest in other games like tennis, which became very popular in the 1400s.

In the United States, interest in sports grew during the 1800s. The English sport of rugby led to the development of Amer-

Lingo to Learn

bye The position of a participant in a tournament who has no opponent after pairs are drawn and who advances to the next round without playing.

contract An agreement between a professional athlete and team management outlining the player's salary, the number of years the player must stay with the team, and other details.

draft The system for dividing up players among professional sports teams.

endorsement An agreement between an athlete and a company, by which the athlete allows the company to use his or her name and image for its advertising in exchange for money.

free agent A professional athlete who is free to negotiate a contract with any team.

scout A professional who attends sporting events in search of new talent.

triathlon An athletic contest in which each competitor takes part in three events: a swimming race, a bicycle race, and a footrace.

ican football, and in 1869, Rutgers and Princeton played the first intercollegiate football game. Many other sports soon followed. Baseball, which stems from the British games of cricket and rounders, was played in its earliest form in 1839 when two teams of schoolboys in Cooperstown, New York, competed in a game of town ball. Town ball, though a popular game, had many problems, the least of which were its lack of standardized rules and the fact that all hits were fair. Players frequently ran directly into one another. Hoping to make improvements, one of the boys, Abner Doubleday, made up rules to a new game, which he called baseball. However, these rules went through many changes and developments before the game became widely accepted and played in the mid-1840s.

Basketball has a more easily traceable history. This sport was invented by Dr. James Naismith, a physical education instructor at the International Young Men's Christian Association Training School in Springfield, Massachusetts (today's Springfield College), in 1891. In the fall Dr. Naismith's students played football outside, and in the spring they returned outside for baseball. But during winter, the students and staff were forced to stay in the gym to do calisthenics and march. Understandably, the students were miserable during these winter activities and complained constantly, so Dr. Naismith decided to find a sport he could adapt to indoor play.

He tried rugby, but his students got hurt tackling each other on the wooden floor. Soccer left too many broken windows in the gym, and at such close quarters the long sticks of lacrosse were causing bruises and worse. About to give up, Naismith turned to the concept of creating a new sport that would fulfill his purposes.

He started with the idea of a ball large enough to eliminate the need for sticks, bats, or other equipment. To keep students from being injured indoors by balls traveling straight at them as in soccer, he

Sport Short

In 1869 Princeton took on Rutgers in the first official football game ever. Twenty-five men played on each side, and Princeton started the game with their new cheer, "Siss! Boom! Ah!" which came from a yell by the Seventh New York Regiment of the Civil War.

decided to raise the goals so that the ball would go in a gentle arc. He found two peach baskets and hung them from 10-foot balconies at each end of the gym. To prevent tackling, he insisted that players not run with the ball. In all, Dr. Naismith's game had 13 rules, and the sport was designed for any number of players. The first game, in December of 1891, had nine men per side shooting at the peach baskets with a soccer ball. Thrilled with the invention, Dr. Naismith's students went home for Christmas break and taught the game to hometown friends. The new sport caught on quickly.

In 1892 Naismith took his students on an exhibition tour of New England, and in 1895, Minnesota State School of Agriculture beat Hamline College 9-3 in the first-ever intercollegiate basketball game. By 1915 the rules to the game had been expanded and standardized, but the game changes even today. Some of the more recent developments in basketball include the shot clock and the three-point shot.

Soon after basketball became popular, golf and tennis were organized into competitive events, and the first championship boxing match was held in New Orleans in 1892.

As the popularity of sports grew, so too did employment opportunities in sports-related occupations. The increasing number and variety of professional sports teams not only created a need for professional athletes, but also introduced an opportunity for coaches, managers, trainers, and scouts. High school and college athletic programs became highly organized, and many additional jobs were created.

The twentieth and twenty-first centuries have seen a rapid growth of sports in the United States—both the professional variety, which emphasizes the business of public entertainment, and amateur and recreational sports, which underscore participation. Professional sports, with their strong spectator appeal, monopolize the sports pages and a large portion of TV programming, especially on weekends. Organized competitive school sports also draw vast audiences of spectators. And the general population is participating in sports of all kinds in unprecedented numbers. Biking, swimming, hiking, skiing, boating, and many other recreational sports have become more and more popular. Golf, traditionally regarded in the United States as the pastime of doctors, bankers, and wealthy retirees, is also rapidly increasing in popularity with the general public.

With the birth of the Women's National Basketball Association (WNBA) and the

Did You Know?

Table tennis was banned in the Soviet Union between 1930 and 1950 because it was thought to be harmful to the eyes.

National Pro Fastpitch League (NPF, softball) and the gold medal–winning U.S. Olympic 1996 softball and 1998 hockey teams, women's sports have becoming increasingly renowned and appreciated. The WNBA and NPF not only offer women athletes new and much-needed venues for participation in professional sports, but also provide many jobs in the industry: coaches, administrators, broadcasters, trainers, referees, umpires, and uniform designers, to name a few.

STRUCTURE OF THE INDUSTRY

In the United States, the five major team sports are baseball, basketball, football, hockey, and soccer. All are structured quite similarly—a good thing to know when planning a job search.

There are also a wide number of sports that require fewer participants. These sports include tennis, golf, boxing, wrestling, horse racing, running, and race car driving.

Most sports teams are owned by one person or a number of people. These owners not only pay the salaries of the athletes and other personnel, but they also often exert a strong influence on the personality of a team. Owners may select athletes who appeal to them and may also set rules and regulations that create a particular atmosphere in the clubhouse or locker room. Owners view their team as a business, and teams may be bought and sold at the discretion of the owner.

Professional team sports are divided into leagues and divisions that act, for administrative purposes, as a subset of the larger sports commission. For example, baseball is divided into the American and National Leagues, and within these leagues further divisions exist. Administrators and other staff members working for sports leagues and divisions are involved in scheduling games and tournament play, reviewing and changing policies and procedures, and hiring league personnel such as umpires.

Sports team employees usually work in one of a few major categories. Many work in an administrative capacity in business, management, and consulting offices. Others work as athletes or with the athletes, and still others are involved in officiating, making sales, providing concessions, and performing many other game-day duties.

Professional sports are divided into seasons. Even though the fans might ignore a sport when it's not being played, most sports league and team employees work for it year-round. Similarly, an actual sporting event may take only a few hours to play, but most workers in the industry arrive several hours early to prepare for the competition and stay well after the contest. Many of the games are

played at night, on weekends, or even on holidays, when the majority of people can attend the contest or watch on TV. There may be a number of games a week or only one or two.

The media have always been an important part of the sports industry. Newspapers, magazines, and the Internet do much to publicize the exploits of the athletes, and live radio broadcasts bring the games to large audiences. Today, television has become the dominant financial factor in professional sports.

Besides the media, the sports industry instersects with a wide variety of other industries as well. Think about all of the companies that design, manufacture, and sell sporting goods, about sports technology, and about all those books of sports statistics. Think about all of the advertising and marketing workers who help attract the public's interest in these sports. Remember that many other fields are involved in sports besides those that might be most obvious.

The structure of non-team sports such as figure skating, golf, and boxing is similar to that of team sports, except, rather than being paid by team owners, employees in the individual sports may earn money from the associations, from prize winnings, from working for special tours and performances, and from endorsements.

The line between amateur and professional sports has begun to blur in recent years. For example, the Olympics was always touted as a venue for amateur athletes, but countries who claimed to have no professional teams always sent their state-supported athletes to compete. In 1992 when the U.S. men's Olympic basketball team, known as the "Dream Team," hit the Barcelona courts with such players as Magic Johnson and Charles Barkley, any notion that the Olympic games were for amateurs disappeared forever.

CAREERS

Careers in professional sports are numerous and varied. Few other industries can match sports in the opportunities it affords someone who wants something new every day. The athlete, or the performer, has the most glamorous position, but managers and other administrative people also play key roles. Radio and television sportscasters, newspaper sportswriters, publicity people, statisticians, officials and umpires, teachers and coaches, attorneys, and scouts all play a major role in presenting a sporting event to the public. A sampling of career opportunities follows below.

Management

The *general manager* is the executive who runs the day-to-day operations of a team. The general manager negotiates player contracts, makes trades with other clubs, and develops a long-range strategy for the team he or she oversees. In these capacities, the general manager works closely with the team's head coach or field manager and with the club's personnel director. The general manager also consults with the *stadium, arena,* or *facility manager*, sometimes called the *stadium oper-* *ations executive,* who is responsible for ticket sales, concessions, security, and other duties. The general manager also needs to know the status of players, and calls on the trainer, team physician, and team surgeon for expert analysis.

Business managers are concerned with making the purchases that keep a team functioning smoothly, such as necessary playing equipment or clubhouse food spreads. They also are responsible for arranging transportation and hotel accommodations when the team travels to another city. On the road, the business manager, sometimes known as the *traveling secretary,* also arranges transportation for media people attached to the club, including newspaper writers and TV reporters.

Athletes, Coaches, Scouts, Agents, and Statisticians

Professional athletes compete for pay as members of a team in such sports as baseball, football, hockey, and basketball, and as individuals in such sports as tennis, figure skating, golf, track, and boxing. Only a very small number of talented athletes ever become professionals. *Sports coaches* work in a broad range of jobs from coaching a school football team to individual tutoring in sports like tennis or golf. There is no limit to how long someone can coach. The idea, however, is to get a coaching start early in one's career because it is a long road up to the premium jobs, and experience counts heavily. Some teachers or coaches are able to communicate best with young people and are completely happy at the high school or college level. Others respond to the challenges and the pressure of the pros, where intricate strategies go hand in hand with high stakes.

Scouts are needed at both the professional and amateur levels to search for talented athletes. They report back to managers and coaches about which players to recruit, draft, trade for, or sign as free agents. Clubs support individual scouting staffs, which are supervised by *head scouts*, and also participate in pool scouting, where one report from a highly skilled scout or team of scouts is furnished to several teams.

Sports agents are employed by athletes to negotiate contracts, obtain endorsements, and handle media requests for interviews.

Statisticians maintain records of the performance of individual athletes and teams. These records change frequently during a contest, so speed and accuracy are at a premium. Since the figures have become more and more sophisticated, statisticians rely heavily on computers. The club's up-to-the-minute statistics may be recalled at a moment's notice, ready to be photocopied for quick distribution in the press box and to other interested parties.

Sports Medicine

The field of sports medicine is a relatively new one that continues to grow. Where athletes once went to general internists and surgeons, doctors are now specializing as sports physicians and sports surgeons, focusing on injuries and medical needs specific to athletes.

Athletic trainers, also called *sports trainers*, *certified sports medicine trainers*, and *certified sports medicine therapists*, are concerned with preventing injuries to amateur and professional athletes through proper exercises and conditioning; providing immediate first aid to injuries if they occur during practice or a competition; and directing injured athletes safely through rehabilitation programs and routines.

Sports Psychology

Sports psychologists work with amateur and professional athletes to improve their mental and physical health as well as athletic performances. Sports psychologists also strive to help athletes mentally prepare for competition. The field of sports psychology is divided into three specialties: clinical, educational, and research. *Clinical sports psychologists* usually work with athletes who are experiencing emotional problems that are usually, but not always, connected to their athletic performance. *Educational sports psychologists* work as classroom instructors to teach students methods and techniques related to sports psychology. They also may serve as a member of a coaching staff. Just as the coach teaches physical skills, this type of sports psychologist teaches mental skills, like positive imaging. *Research sports psychologists* conduct studies that provide the clinical and educational sports psychologists with scientific data and statistics.

Sports Officiating

Sports officials and *umpires* ensure that the rules and regulations of a particular sport are maintained during the course of a contest. They have different responsibilities depending on the type of sport they oversee. *Referees* in tennis, for example, decide when a ball is in or out of play. *Baseball umpires* man each of the three bases and home plate. *Home plate umpires* in baseball determine when a pitched ball is in or out of the strike zone, and they also make calls at the plate. *Boxing referees* watch for illegal punches and signs of fatigue in the fighters. *Track and swimming officials* may use photo-finish technology to determine a winner in an especially close race.

Broadcasting and Journalism

Television and radio announcers describe a contest for at-home viewers and listeners. Announcers come from various backgrounds. Some are ex-athletes, such as Ahmad Rashad and Frank Gifford in football. In basketball, former stars like Julius "Dr. J" Erving have become successful commentators. Some announcers learned the game as college players. Curt Gowdy was a top basketball player at the University of Wyoming; Vin Scully patrolled the outfield for Fordham University's baseball team. Some were professionals in other fields; Howard Cosell decided working in sports was more attractive than practicing law.

Sports journalists may travel with a particular team and report on the successes and failures of the team. They may write articles or broadcast reports about the results of a particular contest or about interesting personalities associated with the team. Sports journalists

with national sports publications cover one or two sports, reviewing the events of competitions across the country and sometimes around the world. *Publicists* arrange interviews with athletes and provide a number of other promotional services to teams. They may run the press box and have other media-related responsibilities.

Most major papers employ *photographers* who specialize in sports. The major wire services operate extensive photographic services with bureaus worldwide. National sports publications normally staff all major events with their own photographers as well. *Stringers*, or photographers who work on a freelance basis for the publication, cover other events.

Technical Production

People with an affinity for electronics may find positions in the technical end of radio or television. Most of these jobs require college training; many two-year technical schools offer training programs specifically for broadcasting. Whether operating a camera, mixing sound in the control truck parked outside the stadium, or giving directions on which part of the action to pick up, the technical staff must know what the equipment can and cannot do.

Facility Design

Sports facility designers are architects and engineers who specialize in the planning, design, and construction of facilities used for sporting and other public events. The buildings that these professionals design may be anything from a community gymnasium to a retractable domed stadium accommodating nearly 100,000 spectators. They consult with clients, plan layouts, prepare drawings of proposed buildings, write specifications, and prepare scale drawings.

Groundskeeping

Grounds managers are responsible for maintaining indoor and outdoor playing fields so that the grass, artificial turf, or clay courts in tennis are in good condition at game time. They may work alone or supervise a staff of grounds workers. They may also be required to alter the stadium for different sports. For example, Chicago's United Center houses both the National Hockey League's Blackhawks and the National Basketball Association's Bulls. So whether it's installing wood flooring over the ice rink or setting up the penalty box, grounds personnel are required to make the sporting event happen.

Groundskeepers are unskilled manual laborers who perform a wide variety of tasks related to a site's maintenance, from hauling tree cuttings to mowing lawns.

Golf course superintendents supervise the construction and maintenance of golf courses and their associated property, including the golf course and practice areas; the golf cart fleet; clubhouse grounds and landscaping; tennis courts, swimming pool, and other recreational facilities; restrooms and potable water on the course; open spaces, wooded areas, unused acreage; and often, the sod farm and nursery.

Concessions and Other Careers

Ushers take tickets, escort spectators to their seats, and provide spectators with information and directions upon request.

Vendors sell a variety of food items and other wares either by walking around and calling out the name of the food or product they're selling, or by operating small booths or kiosks. Sometimes vendors are hired by the food service franchise licensed to sell food in a stadium or sports facility.

As in other industries, there is also a need for administrative workers, such as bookkeepers, secretaries, computer programmers, and marketing and sales workers.

EMPLOYMENT OPPORTUNITIES

There are a wide variety of employment options for those interested in the sports industry. Opportunities exist to do sporting-goods production, athletic

Sport Short

Arguing that the Olympics was for amateur athletes only, the Olympic Committee denied Jim Thorpe his gold medals in 1912 for the pentathlon and decathlon because he had played semipro baseball three years earlier. In 1982 the committee changed its ruling and awarded the medals to Thorpe's children.

performance, broadcasting, officiating, clerical duties, management, marketing, sales, and promotion. Interested people will be able to find positions in the sports industry regardless of their educational achievement or athletic ability. Those with a true love of sports who do not find professional-level employment may choose to work in youth programs as volunteers or paid part-time employees. Officials, coaches, trainers, and scouts are always needed at this level.

Opportunities for employment in sports exist throughout the country. Nearly all major cities have at least one professional sports team. Many slightly smaller cities have minor-league teams and sporting associations. Sports such as tennis, golf, horse racing, and track and field stage frequent competitions in many locations throughout the country and are governed by a variety of administrative organizations and programs.

Sports occupations can also be found at colleges, universities, and junior colleges. Of course, there are many volunteer and part-time sports positions in the high school and youth leagues throughout the country. Truly, there is almost no place in the United States where someone with an interest in sports cannot find some type of employment.

It is the childhood dream of many to become a professional athlete. Most athletes train for many years before becoming professionals. It takes a combination of dedication, physical fitness, talent, experience, and, frankly, plenty of luck to make it to the pros. It is very important for a talented athlete to receive proper coaching early in life to develop an understanding of the fundamentals. College athletics often provide the training ground for athletes who make the transition to professional sports. Some athletes are able to make the transition directly from high school; however, the choice to move directly into professional athletics should not be made lightly. If an athlete's career is short-lived, then he or she has little training for another career and may have to return to school for more education. Oftentimes, athletes who have short professional careers or who have spent considerable time in the minor leagues or at junior levels, focus their know-how and expertise into other related occupations, becoming scouts, coaches, managers, or professional broadcasters. Many may start at the minor league levels of their particular sport, working their way up to the higher levels after considerable experience.

Leagues and associations employ many people in the sports industry. Baseball umpires, for example, are employed by either the American or National League, and not by a specific team. Like teams, leagues and associations also have their own administrators and officials.

If you are interested in sports media, the major employers tend to be radio and television stations and networks, and sports magazines and newspapers, though individual teams do often have their own broadcasters, publicists, and other media personnel on staff. Sportswriters are usually college educated with a major in journalism, English, creative writing, communications, or some other

Success Story

The runners sprint toward the finish line, two of them together in the lead. Twenty meters to go. Fifteen. Ten. Their leg muscles bulge, chests pound, lungs swell with oxygen. As the runners put on a final burst of speed, the crowd stands to see the two leading racers break the tape neck in neck. A tie . . . . Or is it?

The evolution of timing technology in sports has changed the industry forever. Winners in the earliest contests were determined simply by the human eye; who was perceived to arrive first? In 1900, for example, American Francis Jarvis was officially recorded as the winner of the 100 meters as "the winner by one foot from Walter Tewksbury, who beat Australian Stan Rowley by inches."

In 1932 the stopwatch and camera appeared at the Olympic games in Los Angeles. The camera was used to determine a winner after the human eye and the stopwatch could not separate runners Ralph Metcalfe and Eddie Tolan. The judges watched the camera's film and after several hours decided that Tolan had won.

Early cameras and stopwatches were accurate only to one-tenth of a second at best. This may sound precise enough, but remember that in the world of professional sports, athletes may be so evenly matched that they finish less than one-tenth of a second apart, an amount of time that those older devices could not distinguish. Furthermore, the several hours it could take judges to review the film held up the event.

The field of sports technology continues to work to solve these problems. Among the latest advancements in the field is the computerized digital photo finish system. With this technology, several cameras relay immediate information to a timer that is connected to a computer. This computer allows judges to discern a winner instantly down to one-thousandth of a second difference!

area that trains the student in communication skills. Knowledge of sports is essential. Working on college newspapers, stringing (working on a freelance basis) for newspapers, and taking advantage of any sportswriting opportunities while in school are recommended.

Radio and television broadcasters should have an interest in sports and a dedication to the spoken word and how language affects others. Radio and television are for people who can say something well and in a manner that holds the attention of listeners. In addition, a candidate should be comfortable in front of a camera. Some on-air sportscasters have journalism training; however, others have had no formal education but have developed a talent for on-air coverage. Portfolios, clips, tapes, or videos are usually requested by employers to demonstrate competency in sports coverage.

People interested in sports equipment and apparel design are usually employed by the manufacturers of these goods. These workers may have a background in such wide-ranging fields as textiles, fashion, physics, or athletics. For example, many designers of today's elite mountain bikes are themselves mountain bikers. Most workers in this field apply directly to the company for whom they would like to work.

Managers, administrators, and administrative staff are hired and employed by all teams, leagues, and sports associations at every level.

INDUSTRY OUTLOOK

The greatest number of job opportunities exists with professional teams. There are more than 145 professional football, baseball, hockey, soccer, and basketball teams on the major-league level.

The number of professional teams, in all sports, is relatively stable. This means, however, that the number of jobs is also relatively stable. For jobs that are specifically sports-related, such as managers, coaches, umpires, and referees, job openings appear as people retire or otherwise leave the profession. Jobs also emerge with the birth of expansion teams, such as the Arizona Diamondbacks, which joined professional baseball in 1998, and the less common advent of new leagues or sports, such as the WNBA and the NPF.

For occupations that are also related to other fields, such as journalists, publicists, business managers, and attorneys, there is some movement of trained individuals into and out of the sports sector. The competition for all these jobs is fairly keen. The number of people interested in working in sports far exceeds the number of openings.

As difficult as it is to get a nonathletic position, the competition for a job as a professional athlete is much tougher. In college football, for example, there are more than 120 Division I football teams and countless other teams in other divisions—but only 32 professional football teams in the National Football League.

Few of the college athletes who wish to make the pros will be chosen. Of those chosen, many will not last the season; others will not play for more than a couple of years. Few professional football players are able to make a career of the sport. The same is true for other sports. Golf, tennis, and other individual sports enable professionals to play at the international level; however, the financial incentive for players who do not win tournaments is limited. Only a few players will earn the large incomes of athletes on the level of Tiger Woods or Serena Williams.

As the field of technology grows, so do its applications in the sports industry. Programmers are needed to improve computer-based timing equipment, while other workers in sports technology may be needed for designing more aerodynamic bicycles and creating swimming pools with minimal wave interference.

Sports medicine is a relatively new addition to the industry and has good growth potential. Sports doctors and surgeons are beginning to specialize in the injuries particular to athletes, and more and more teams and athletes are employing massage and physical therapists, chiropractors and kinesiologists, sports nutritionists, and skilled trainers. In addition, there has been a recent boom in written information on health and sports medicine, including many books and magazines that focus specifically on these issues.

SECTION 2

Careers

Athletic Trainers

SUMMARY

Definition
Athletic trainers help amateur and professional athletes prevent injuries, give first aid when an injury occurs during a practice or event, and manage the rehabilitation programs and routines of injured athletes.

Alternative Job Titles
Athletic trainers

Certified sports medicine therapists
Certified sports medicine trainers
Sports trainers

Salary Range
$19,750 to $45,000 to $125,000

Educational Requirements
Bachelor's degree

Certification or Licensing
Recommended

Employment Outlook
Much faster than the average

High School Subjects
Health
Physical education

Personal Interests
Exercise/personal fitness
Helping people: physical health/medicine
Sports

"Picking the most interesting thing that has happened in my work as an athletic trainer is like asking which of my children I love the most," says Bruce Fischbach, head athletic trainer at the University of South Dakota (USD). "It is impossible to answer. Mostly I have a collage of memories of student-athletes, as they score touchdowns, shoot baskets, and come to the finish line overcoming the injury obstacle that had been placed in their way. It is a tremendous high as they come off the field of competition and find *you* to thank *you* for helping them achieve their goal!"

WHAT DO ATHLETIC TRAINERS DO?

Athletic trainers help amateur and professional athletes prevent injuries through proper exercise and conditioning; provide immediate first aid attention to injuries as they occur during a practice or event; and lead injured athletes safely through rehabilitation programs and routines. (For the purposes of this book, the term *athletic trainer* refers to certified athletic trainers who have received specialized training and passed a certification exam.) For the most part, athletic trainers are not medical doctors, and are not allowed to conduct certain procedures or provide advanced types of medical care, such as prescribing or administering drugs. Some athletic trainers, however, are trained physicians. If an individual is also trained as an osteopathic physician, for example, he or she is licensed as a medical doctor and can conduct more advanced procedures and techniques, including diagnosis, surgery, and the prescription of drugs.

In order to prevent injuries, athletic trainers organize team physicals, making certain that each player is examined and evaluated by a physician prior to that athlete's participation in the sport. Along with the team physician, they help to analyze each athlete's overall readiness to play, fitness level, and known or existing weaknesses or injuries. When necessary, they recommend stretching, conditioning, and strengthening exercises to aid the athlete in preventing or exacerbating an injury. This may involve developing specific routines for individual athletes. Finally, athletic trainers work with coaches, and sometimes team physicians, to choose protective athletic equipment. Before games and practice, they often inspect the playing field, surface, or area for any flagrant or subtle risks of injury to the athletes.

Prior to a practice or competition, the athletic trainer may help an athlete conduct special stretching exercises or, as a preventive measure, he or she might tape, wrap, bandage, or brace knees, ankles, or other joints, and areas of the athlete's body that might be at risk for injury. The athletic trainer routinely treats cuts, scratches, abrasions, and other minor injuries. He or she may tape, pad, or wrap injuries and install face guards. When serious injuries do occur, whether in practice or during a competition, the athletic trainer's role is to provide prompt and accurate first aid treatment to the athlete to ensure that athlete's full recovery. He or she is trained in emergency procedures and is prepared to provide emergency treatment for conditions such as shock, concussion, or bone fracture, stabilizing the athlete until he or she reaches a hospital or trauma center. Often, the athletic trainer accompanies the injured athlete to the hospital, provided that the team physician is on hand to address the health concerns and needs of those athletes who are still competing.

Working in concert with the team physician and several other health professionals, athletic trainers often supervise the therapeutic rehabilitation of athletes under their care. They analyze the athlete's injury and create individualized therapy routines. Sometimes, the athletic trainer may advise the athlete to wear a protective brace or guard to minimize damage while the athlete is recuperating from an injury. Athletic trainers in charge of every level of athlete should be licensed to perform specific medical functions and operate certain devices and equipment.

Athletes train year-round, so the athletic trainers who supervise their conditioning and rehabilitation programs work year-round as well. Depending on the level and size of an athletic program, athletic trainers may work with athletes in one or more sports. Athletic trainers who work in high schools often act as the care provider for several, or all, of the athletic teams. A lot also depends on the school's budgetary restrictions. Generally speaking, though, most schools have a separate individual for men's and women's sports. Athletic trainers in professional sports work only in one sport and for one team.

Most of the athletic trainer's time is spent in the school's athletic facility, either in making preparations or in conditioning or rehab sessions. Athletic trainers are on a schedule similar to that of their athletes; they go to practices, schedule weight and rehab sessions, and attend games. They are expected to travel when and where the team travels.

WHAT IS IT LIKE TO BE AN ATHLETIC TRAINER?

Bruce Fischbach has been a certified athletic trainer since July 1985, and has served as the head athletic trainer at the University of South Dakota since September 1987. "This is a tremendous field in which to have a career," he says. "I find it very hard to say I am 'going to work' because I love this profession."

The University of South Dakota sponsors 17 sports, with more than 500 total student-athletes (SAs) competing, and Bruce says that they all place differing demands on the sports medicine team. "Our sports are varied in that some are outdoor sports (football, cross country, soccer, softball, track and field, golf,

and tennis), while others are more traditionally indoors (swimming, basketball, and volleyball). The University of South Dakota has as its athletic headquarters the DakotaDome, a multiuse facility that allows all of our teams to practice indoors if the weather is bad. We do play our home football games inside."

Bruce's day typically begins at 8:00 A.M. "We ask that all of our injured SAs receive treatments three times per day," he says, "once in the morning and pre- and post-practice. So we do treatments in the morning, as well as teach sports medicine classes for the Division of Health, Physical Education and Recreation here at USD." In addition to these tasks, Bruce also spends the morning working on insurance claims, handling budgeting and inventory issues, answering e-mails, and performing other administrative tasks.

During the afternoon, Bruce prepares the SAs for practice, gives treatments to the injured, and implements possible preventive or supportive measures (taping) for the noninjured and injured. "Some members of our staff," he says, "then follow the SAs to practice to monitor the injured SAs as they try to practice and watch for injuries to occur and render aid as needed. Following practice, it is once again treatment time. This day, during a football season, can last until 7:00 P.M.!"

When an athletic team from the university travels, at least one member of the sports medicine team also travels with the team. "The sports medicine team may travel with several certified athletic trainers if the team has a large roster," Bruce says. "For example, when the football team travels, four certified athletic trainers make the trip. As a member of the travel squad, I have traveled all over the United States (both coasts, Disney World, Travel has also included trips outside the United States to foreign countries. Once again, if a USD athletic team travels, we go with!"

DO I HAVE WHAT IT TAKES TO BE AN ATHLETIC TRAINER?

Workers in this field need an understanding of human anatomy and physiology, both in terms of physical capabilities and injury treatment and prevention. They should not be squeamish when it comes to blood, broken bones, or other wounds. Athletes do get hurt, and an athletic trainer who is unable to cope well with this aspect of sports may have a difficult time succeeding in the career. The ability

To Be a Successful Athletic Trainer, You Should . . .

- have an understanding of human anatomy and physiology

- not be squeamish when it comes to blood, broken bones, or other wounds

- be levelheaded and decisive during emergencies

- have strong communication skills

and knowledge to handle medical emergencies is especially important for certified athletic trainers, whose work focuses on injury prevention and treatment.

HOW DO I BECOME AN ATHLETIC TRAINER?

Education

High School

If you have an interest in becoming an athletic trainer, you've probably already become involved in the field during high school. Maybe you're not an athlete but you work as a student trainer or manager for one of your school teams. These are excellent ways to develop your interest in sports, learn about the skills that athletic trainers must have, and develop the leadership abilities necessary for the job.

If you're interested in this field, you should pay special attention to physical education classes and to high school subjects such as health and anatomy and physiology. Students with an interest in becoming athletic trainers need to become certified in CPR and first aid.

Postsecondary Training

Athletic trainers must earn a bachelor's degree from a college or university offering a program in athletic training that is accredited by the Commission on Accreditation of Allied Health Education Programs (upon the recommendation of the Commission on Accreditation of Athletic Training Education, http://www.jrc-at.org). Bruce received his undergraduate degree from the University of Nebraska–Lincoln.

Many employers are now requiring applicants to have a master's degree in athletic training or a related field. According to the National Athletic Trainers' Association, 70 percent of athletic trainers today have a master's or higher degree. "Most certified athletic trainers do hold advanced degrees," Bruce says. "My master's degree is from the United States Sports Academy in Daphne, Alabama."

All accredited programs in athletic training include course work in the prevention and evaluation of athletic injuries and illnesses, first aid and emergency care, therapeutic exercises, therapeutic modalities, administration of athletic training programs, human anatomy, human physiology, exercise physiology, kinesiology, nutrition, psychology, and personal and community health.

Certification or Licensing

As mentioned earlier, athletic trainers in charge of every level of athlete should be licensed to perform specific medical functions and operate certain devices and equipment. Different membership organizations and their respective certifying bodies have different eligibility requirements; it is up to you to decide which organization best characterizes your ultimate goal.

For example, the National Athletic Trainers' Association (NATA) requires that those seeking certification have graduated from an entry-level Commission on Accreditation of Allied Health Education

The Pros and Cons of Being an Athletic Trainer

The editors of *What Can I Do Now?: Sports* asked Bruce Fischbach, head athletic trainer at the University of South Dakota, to tell us what he likes most and least about his job.

Pros

- I receive front-row seats to every University of South Dakota sports contest (home and away).

- You get the opportunity to be a part of a "team."

- It is a thrill to see an injured student-athlete (SA) return to competition and know that in some small way you helped this happen.

Cons:

- The long hours can sometimes be tedious.

- When our teams play, we are there, including holidays and weekends.

Programs–accredited athletic training curriculum and pass a certification exam consisting of three sections—written, simulation (situations designed to approximate real-life athletic training challenges), and oral practical (to evaluate skill components).

Approximately 43 states require some form of certification, licensure, or registration for athletic trainers. For more information, check with the regulatory agency in the state in which you would like to practice for more information.

Internships and Volunteerships

During your college training, you will be required to participate in an internship, which will last between one and two semesters. During your internship, you might get the opportunity to work as an assistant to an athletic trainer in a sports program at a college or university or to work with trainers in a health care setting. Internships are usually nonpaying; instead of financial remuneration, interns receive credit hours for their work.

High school and college students can gain valuable experience by actively participating in a sport. Such experience lends a prospective trainer added insight into the injuries typical of a given sport, as well as the compassion and empathy necessary to comfort an injured athlete who is forced to sit out a game. Most teams need help with everything from equipment to statistics, so plenty of opportunities exist to explore a variety of sports-related positions. If you are certain about your decision to become an athletic trainer, you can often work with an athletic trainer or team physician, learning beside a professional. This type of experience will come in handy later, when you are looking for an internship or a job; successful candidates are usually those with the most experience and on-the-job training.

WHO WILL HIRE ME?

Approximately 15,000 athletic trainers are employed in the United States. Athletic trainers are hired by the wide variety of teams and sports requiring coaches, from high school to the pros; however, their means of entrance is slightly different. Certified athletic trainers who focus on injury prevention and treatment may apply directly to teams or sports for which they want to work. Often, experience, certification credentials, and recommendations play a large role in helping athletic trainers gain desired positions.

Athletic trainers interested in working in a gym setting should apply at fitness centers, the YMCA or Jewish Community Center, or racquet, golf, and swim clubs. Recently, many large companies and office complexes have begun creating exercise facilities for employees on-site, and they hire professional athletic trainers to assist with purchasing equipment and teaching people to use it, as well as developing individual fitness regimens and instructing on injury prevention. Many ambulatory heath care services, offices of physicians, offices of other health practitioners, and hospital wellness centers—basically hospital-run gymnasiums—also employ athletic trainers to assist people with rehabilitation or with staying fit. In fact, 33 percent of athletic trainers are employed in these settings.

WHERE CAN I GO FROM HERE?

Acquiring additional training and education is the most common way of advancing in the field of athletic training. Those athletic trainers who have spent years working in the field and who update their skills each year by taking continuing education courses, sometimes even returning to school for an advanced degree, will be among the first to receive promotions.

Managerial responsibilities also allow athletic trainers to advance in their field. Large universities often employ several athletic trainers to serve the many different teams, with one athletic trainer acting as the *head athletic trainer*, sometimes also called the *director of sports medicine*. This individual coordinates the daily activities and responsibilities of the other athletic trainers and works closely with the coaches of the school's various teams to ensure that all the demands are being met. Most often, athletic trainers advance by working for several years at one school, and then move on to another school when an opening is announced that will afford greater responsibilities and benefits.

As head athletic trainer at USD, Bruce has reached the top of the athletic training career ladder at the university. "While I have held the same job for the past 19 years," he says, "it has evolved and it constantly changes. At the collegiate level, we continually change our rosters as we recruit many and graduate others. We are also growing here at the university. In 1987, we had approximately 250 SAs, and our numbers have grown to over 550 as we have added sports and rosters have increased. Additionally, to meet the demands of more and more sports and SAs, our sports medicine staff has grown. I came to USD thinking that it was a nice place to start a career, and now I think it would be a great place from which to retire!"

WHAT ARE THE SALARY RANGES?

Earnings vary depending on the level of athletics in which the athletic trainer is involved, the athletic trainer's education and credentials, and the number and type of his or her responsibilities. Those considering a career as an athletic trainer should keep all aspects of the job and salary in perspective; the slight increase in salary of an athletic trainer working for a college team might be offset by the higher stress levels and longer hours away from home. Athletic trainers who work with professional athletes are away from home a great deal, including evenings, weekends, and holidays.

According to the National Association for Sport and Physical Education, salaries for athletic trainers in schools range from $25,000 to $35,000. With experience and a master's degree, college athletic trainers can earn up to $45,000 to $60,000 per

Related Jobs

- emergency medical technicians
- nurses
- nutritionists
- physical education teachers
- physical therapists
- physical therapy assistants and aides
- physician assistants
- recreation workers
- sports physicians and surgeons

year. Athletic trainers who work for professional sports teams earn salaries ranging from $60,000 to $125,000.

The U.S. Department of Labor reports that athletic trainers earned median salaries of $33,590 in 2004. The highest 10 percent earned more than $53,970, while the lowest 10 percent earned less than $19,750.

WHAT IS THE JOB OUTLOOK?

Depending on the setting in which the athletic trainer is involved, the employment outlook varies. The outlook is best for athletic trainers employed in health care settings such as ambulatory health care services and hospitals. In the sports industry, the outlook is slightly less positive than it is for athletic trainers employed in health care; positions with professional athletes and teams are extremely difficult to find, and those working in them usually have years and years of experience. More opportunities exist for certified athletic trainers who work with high school athletes, especially if athletic trainers have other skills that make them more employable. For example, the athletic trainer wishing to work with high school athletes who also can teach biology, math, physical education, or other school subjects most likely will find a position sooner than the candidate with only a background in athletic training. The reasoning is simple: with school budgets being cut back, those individuals who perform double-duty will be more attractive to school boards looking to cut costs.

Competition for positions at the college and university level is also tough, and many schools are now requiring candidates to have a master's degree in order to be considered.

Grounds Managers and Groundskeepers

SUMMARY

Definition
Grounds managers are members of a management team that is responsible for the maintenance of a wide variety of sports playing fields, as well as other public and private sites. Working under the supervision of grounds managers is a crew of groundskeepers, unskilled laborers who work to maintain a site's appearance.

Alternative Job Titles
Sports field managers
Sports turf managers
Turfgrass managers

Salary Range
$35,000 to $57,000 to $110,000 (grounds managers)
$14,000 to $20,000 to $33,000+ (groundskeepers)

Educational Requirements
Bachelor's degree (grounds managers)
High school diploma (groundskeepers)

Certification or Licensing
Required for certain positions

Employment Outlook
Faster than the average

High School Subjects
Earth science
Mathematics

Personal Interests
Sports

Mike Andresen, athletic turf manager for Iowa State University, says that good communication skills may be as important, or even more important, than agronomic skills for success in this profession. "My job requires regular communications with high-energy coaches and administrators," he explains. "Maintenance programs oftentimes conflict with coaches' demands for our facilities. I'm very fortunate at Iowa State to have coaches who respect and appreciate the challenges our crew faces day in and day out. They appreciate that we play a role in maintaining safe fields for their athletes, and that our mission includes providing them the highest-quality surfaces to compete on and to recruit to. We are part of their teams, and we want to help great athletes be able to make great plays on our fields."

WHAT DO GROUNDS MANAGERS AND GROUNDSKEEPERS DO?

Within the sports industry, *grounds managers* and *groundskeepers* work to maintain the condition of the playing fields and of the lands surrounding the related facilities. For example, grounds managers and groundskeepers are hired to keep both natural and artificial turf areas in top condition for the sport played there. In addition to planting the proper type of natural turf or laying artificial turf and ensuring that it has excellent drainage, groundsworkers regularly mow, fertilize, and aerate the fields. They spray protective pesticides on natural turf to control weeds, kill pests, and prevent diseases or insect infestations from destroying the field's appearance.

Even artificial turf requires special care; grounds managers and their crews must vacuum and disinfect it after a sporting event so that harmful bacteria won't grow and destroy the turf or harm the players who compete on the field. Periodically, the cushioning pad beneath the artificial turf must be replaced. Part of the care for the playing fields includes painting the appropriate boundaries, markers, and team logos and names on the turf, and sometimes even retouching them during sporting events.

Grounds managers and groundskeepers also maintain the ornamental grasses, shrubs, plants, and flowers on the grounds of a football stadium, baseball park, or general sports arena. In general, this means they are responsible for planting, pruning, mowing, transplanting, fertilizing, spraying, trimming, training, edging, and any other duties that will keep the landscape looking healthy and attractive. They may work year-round to ensure the quality of the playing fields and other grounds. In certain regions of the country, the grounds manager may need to hire extra groundskeepers during peak periods and cut staff during slower months. In general, spring and summer are the peak seasons, while autumn and winter are much slower. However, schedules depend on the site where grounds managers and groundskeepers work. For example, fall and winter are the busiest times of the year for the groundsworkers who maintain the field of a National Football League team.

Golf is the only major sport in which the playing field does not conform to specific dimensions or characteristics. In fact, the varying natural features of each course present the golfer with many of the sport's challenges. As a result, the diverse areas of the golf course require that the individuals caring for it have a wide range of knowledge and expertise in everything from plants to ponds. On golf courses, landscapers and grounds managers are employed as *greenskeepers*. There are two types of greenskeepers: *Greenskeepers I* supervise and coordinate the activities of workers engaged in keeping the grounds and turf of a golf course in good playing condition. They consult with the greens superintendent to plan and review work projects; they determine work assignments, such as fertilizing, irrigating, seeding, mowing, raking, and spraying; and they mix and prepare spraying and dusting solutions. They may also repair and maintain mechanical equipment.

Greenskeepers II follow the instructions of Greenskeepers I as they maintain the grounds of golf courses. They cut the turf on green and tee areas; dig and rake grounds to prepare and cultivate new greens; connect hose and sprinkler systems; plant trees and shrubs; and operate tractors as they apply fertilizer, insecticide, and other substances to the fairways or other designated areas.

Golf Facts

• • • • •

- Golf was invented in Scotland in the 1500s.

- The Professional Golfers' Association of America was founded in 1916 at the Taplow Club in New York City.

- The first golf cart was invented in the 1940s. It was created solely to help people with disabilities enjoy the game of golf.

- More than 25 million people play golf at one of the more than 17,000 golf courses in the United States annually.

- It is estimated that the golf industry generates $20 billion in annual revenue.

- Environmental benefits of healthy golf courses include the production of oxygen, the cooling of the atmosphere, the prevention of erosion, the filtering of contaminants from rainfall and irrigation, and the preservation of "greenspace," especially in urban settings. Golf courses also provide a sanctuary to wildlife, recreational areas for non-golfing-related activities, and job opportunities for a variety of workers.

Sources: Professional Golfers' Association of America, Golf Course Superintendents Association of America

---

Greens superintendents supervise and coordinate the activities of greenskeepers and other workers engaged in constructing and maintaining golf course areas. They review test results of soil and turf samples, and they direct the application of fertilizer, lime, insecticide, or fungicide. Their other duties include monitoring the course grounds to determine the need for irrigation or better care, keeping and reviewing maintenance records, and interviewing and hiring workers.

In addition to the "green" side of the job, grounds managers fulfill specific supervisory duties, such as managing finances, materials, equipment, and staff needed to maintain a playing field and related facilities. For most managers, this means developing goals, scheduling maintenance operations, assigning staff hours, creating budgets, delegating tasks, conducting cost accounting procedures, and hiring, training, and supervising employees.

WHAT IS IT LIKE TO BE A GROUNDS MANAGER OR GROUNDSKEEPER?

Mike Andresen has been the athletic turf manager for Iowa State University for 10 years. His responsibilities consist of managing the buildings and grounds department for the university's intercollegiate athletic department. Prior to taking this job, Mike was head groundskeeper for the Iowa Cubs minor league baseball team for five years. And before that, he worked in various turfgrass and landscape management/maintenance capacities in the green industry.

Mike says that a normal day for a sports turf manager varies from facility to facility and region to region. "During an Iowa winter," he explains, "a normal day will consist of equipment maintenance, budgeting, or setting up for a high-quality indoor track meet.

"During spring we may host a Big XII Conference softball game, a tennis meet, a spring football practice, and a soccer practice all on the same day, and we'll turn around the next day and do it all over again.

"Summer has our facilities hosting youth camps and special events (Special Olympics Festival, Iowa Games festival, etc.). Summer is the time when our heavier maintenance programs occur, such as aeration and topdressing. Schedules are made well in advance to be able to accommodate proper maintenance and busy event schedules.

"During fall, our attention flips as football and soccer have their competitive seasons and the other sports move to off-season practicing. Fall is our busiest season and is when public exposure to our facilities is greatest, both from fans and media. Working overtime is a must, though we subscribe to the 'work smarter, not harder' philosophy. Weather is constantly on our mind and dictates much of our daily work schedule. If playing fields need painting and rain is in the forecast, we have to decide on the fly how we will change our schedule to ensure the fields will play and look their finest for the event." Mike says that he accrues most of his overtime during spring and fall—his busiest seasons.

DO I HAVE WHAT IT TAKES TO BE A GROUNDS MANAGER OR GROUNDSKEEPER?

To be a successful grounds manager, you should have good organizational, communication, and leadership skills. "Managing a crew of any size takes skill and commitment," Mike says, "and only comes with experience and the realization that you will be judged as a manager by how successful you are in maintaining a motivated and skilled staff. Being self motivated is also a very important key to being successful. Few people in our athletic department know what it takes to achieve success in our profession, day to day. Sports field managers need to be able to organize the field needs and blend them into short-term and long-term programs to achieve success."

Grounds managers and groundskeepers for sports facilities are usually under a lot of pressure to complete a job in time for a sports event. Often these sports events are televised, making it that much more important for the football field or baseball diamond to look well cared for. "Being able to perform under pressure is key to having success in this profession," Mike says.

Grounds managers and their crews frequently work with pesticides, herbicides, fungicides, and other chemicals, and it is essential that they observe safety precautions when applying these chemicals in order to prevent exposure. Similarly, grounds managers and their crews use many different tools and machines to complete their tasks, from driving a truck

To Be a Successful Grounds Manager, You Should . . .

- have good organizational skills
- be an excellent communicator
- have strong leadership and management skills
- be able to work under deadline pressure
- have vision regarding the short- and long-term needs of your facility

or lawn mower, to operating power clippers, chain saws, and sod cutters.

Groundskeepers must be able to follow directions and be responsible, since they are often assigned duties and then asked to work without direct supervision.

To Be a Successful Groundskeeper, You Should . . .

- be able to work under deadline pressure
- be able to follow directions
- be able to work without direct supervision
- have good communication skills
- be physically fit

HOW DO I BECOME A GROUNDS MANAGER OR GROUNDSKEEPER?

Education

Mike says that he has always been passionate about athletics and athletic performance. "In high school I worked part time at the local golf course doing course maintenance," he says. "After high school, I was fortunate to play college baseball at a school where the team members were required to do much of the field maintenance on our facility. After realizing my baseball career had topped out, I fell back to a love of maintaining turf in general, with a focus on athletic fields specifically." At this point, Mike decided to attend a community college with a strong horticulture program to learn turf and horticulture. "After graduation," he recalls, "I dove headlong into a turf and landscape management career, always with a dream that I would end up maintaining some level of athletic facilities. Even then, I realized that working passionately was the pathway to long-term success in any profession and my two passions were, and still are, athletics and turf management."

High School

Though there are no formal educational requirements for becoming a groundskeeper, grounds managers must have a solid educational background to prepare them for a college program. While in high school, study chemistry, biology, and earth science, as well as English, foreign languages, and mathematics. Managers need solid communication skills to work well with their crews and need mathematical ability to balance their budgets and keep other records.

Postsecondary Training

Those interested in becoming grounds managers should aim for a bachelor of science in grounds management, horticulture, turfgrass management, agronomy, or a related field. In addition, most employers require that managers have a minimum of four years of experience, with at least two in a supervisory position. Grounds managers need to be comfortable with budgeting, management, and cost-accounting procedures, to possess public relations and communication skills, and to be current with maintenance issues, such as recycling and hazardous materials. Courses in business management and personnel management are very helpful, although not required.

Most groundskeeping jobs do not require a college degree. Many people working these jobs are either looking to get on-the-job experience or simply trying to make a little extra money. However, some positions involving the application of pesticides, fungicides, and other chemicals do require some educational training.

Certification and Training

The Sports Turf Managers Association offers the Certified Sports Field Manager (CSFM) designation to applicants who meet educational and/or experience requirements and pass an examination that covers agronomics, pest management, administration, and sports-specific field management. Mike earned the CSFM designation in 2000. "Becoming certified is important in our profession in many ways," he says, "and as the program increases in size, the athletic community will recognize that a CSFM is good assurance that a facility is managed by a competent professional."

Landscapers and grounds managers who specialize in the care of golf courses and sports fields can receive certification from the Golf Course Superintendents Association of America or the Sports Turf Managers Association.

In addition, the Professional Landcare Network offers the following voluntary certification designations: Certified Landscape Technician (Exterior and Interior), Certified Landscape Professional, Certified Ornamental Landscape Professional, Certified Turfgrass Professional, and Certified Turfgrass Professional–Cool Season Lawns. All certification tests are multiple choice and cover landscaping skills as well as some business and management topics.

The Professional Grounds Management Society also offers certification for both grounds managers (the Certified Grounds Manager certification) and for groundsworkers (the Certified Grounds Technician certification).

In the interest of public safety, some states require groundsworkers to pass a certification examination on the proper application of pesticides, fungicides, and other harsh chemicals.

Contractors and other self-employed people may also need a license to operate their businesses.

Internships and Volunteerships

Most college students participate in an internship with a professional or amateur sports team, recreational facility, nursery, botanical garden, or park. Internships typically last from 4 to 12 months. They are excellent methods of learning about the different careers in grounds management.

Volunteer or part-time groundskeeping positions are excellent ways for high school students to gain valuable experience in the field. Prior work in a grounds crew can help you later when you are pursuing a career in grounds management. Because most groundskeeping positions are seasonal, you can volunteer or work part time after school and on weekends during the school year, and full time during the summer. Interested students should start by contacting the municipal parks district, lawn care companies, nurseries, botanical gardens, and professional landscapers in their area to inquire about job possibilities.

WHO WILL HIRE ME?

Mike landed his first job as a sports turf manager when he was hired as head groundskeeper for the Iowa Cubs baseball team, the Triple A affiliate of the Chicago Cubs. "Securing this job was my dream come true," he says, "and I poured my heart and soul into being a successful sports turf manager and crew manager. When I took the Iowa Cubs job, I had 12 years of experience in turf management from previous jobs, and had donated my time and skills to working on all levels of athletic fields whenever possible." Mike played baseball with the general manager of the Iowa Cubs, so landing the job as head groundskeeper for the Iowa Cubs, he says, "was very much about 'who you know' and being prepared for the opportunity if it ever came! I needed a fortunate 'break' to help my dream happen, but I also knew it would be a blessing, and I'd better be prepared to succeed if and when it ever came. That break did happen, I was determined to have it change my life for the better, and it has!"

There are approximately 1.5 million groundsworkers currently employed in the United States. Managers and supervisors hold 184,000 jobs; groundskeepers hold approximately 1.17 million jobs. Depending on their experience prior to receiving a degree in agronomy or horticulture, candidates for management positions can start in an entry-level groundskeeping job. Working in a nursery, botanical garden, or park offers the opportunity to learn about the care of plants, flowers, trees, and shrubs. A summer job may evolve into a full-time supervisory position following graduation from a four-year program.

Summer or part-time jobs as groundskeepers often lead to full-time employment with the same employer. Those who enroll in a college or other training programs can receive help in finding work from the school's career services office. In addition, directly applying to botanical gardens, nurseries, or golf courses is common practice. Jobs may also be listed in newspaper want ads. Most landscaping and related companies provide on-the-job training for entry-level personnel.

In addition to employment at sports-related facilities, groundsworkers are employed at public parks and recreation areas, apartment complexes, cemeteries, condominiums, estates, schools and universities, shopping centers and malls, theme parks, zoos, commercial and industrial parks, hospitals, airports, and military installations. Cities, towns, and sporting facilities also employ their own groundsmanagement workers. Grounds managers may have their own business or work for one or more landscaping companies.

WHERE CAN I GO FROM HERE?

Advancement usually comes with increased expertise from on-the-job experience (especially in a supervisory position) and additional courses in botany, agronomy, horticulture, and pesticide application. Two- and four-year programs in grounds management, landscape management, turfgrass management, and ornamental horticulture are widely available.

Groundskeepers who acquire additional education and experience can easily advance into management positions. Even a two-year degree can accelerate a groundskeeper's advancement to a supervisory position.

Mike is very happy with his current job, "although my outlook," he says, "is to always be prepared to take on the next challenge, whether it is at my present facility or another one. Money is not the driving force behind my choice of profession, nor is the allure of working in a high-profile job. Finding a professionally challenging position in sports turf management is very rewarding. A natural progression for a person in my position might be to move into facility management, athletic field construction, athletic administration, or countless other positions in the turf, athletic, or recreation industry."

WHAT ARE THE SALARY RANGES?

Salaries for grounds managers vary depending on level of education, training, and experience. According to a survey by the Professional Grounds Management Society (http://www.pgms.org), the average hourly rate for managers/superintendents was $27.89 in 2004. Wages ranged from a low of $21.87 to $30.59 an hour.

The hourly wages for groundskeepers are much lower. Most groundskeepers can only expect to make between $7 and $10 an hour, or roughly $14,720 to $20,670 a year. The most experienced groundskeepers can earn up to $16 an hour, or $33,410 a year. The low wages are one reason why these jobs are often hard to keep filled, with groundskeeping staff continually leaving to find better-paying work.

The *Chicago Tribune* reports that earnings for groundskeepers employed with a sports team to care for the home stadium are much higher. In the early 2000s, the head groundskeeper for the Chicago White Sox reported earning between $45,000 and $110,000 a year. However, he also reported working up to 110-hour weeks when the Sox were in town!

WHAT IS THE JOB OUTLOOK?

Employment of groundskeeping professionals is expected to grow at a faster rate than the average for all occupations through 2014, according to the U.S. Department of Labor. Professional sports arenas, stadiums, and fields and the athletes who play in these venues generate billions of dollars. The appearance of a playing field is extremely important to the team and the community that supports it. Fans and sports management alike take great pride in the way their baseball stadium looks, for example, when it is televised in a national broadcast. Grounds managers and their crews will always remain a vital part of maintaining a sports team's image.

In addition to opportunities in professional sports, turf managers are needed to oversee facilities at golf and country clubs, public parks and recreation areas, athletic fields at schools and universities, and many other settings. "Mid-sized cities all over the country are building youth complexes that need professional management," Mike says. "Many more facilities are expanding or being renovated to handle increased numbers of events and competitions. Administrators, parents, and field managers all have prioritized that having safe fields for athletes to compete on is our highest calling. Because of the importance we've placed on this, our industry will continue to offer great opportunities for progressive managers for years to come."

Related Jobs

- arborists
- forestry technicians
- horticultural technicians
- landscape architects
- landscapers
- lawn and gardening service owners

Professional Athletes

SUMMARY

Definition
Professional athletes compete in athletic events for prizes and salaries and to entertain fans.

Alternative Job Titles
None

Salary Range
$14,000 to $39,000 to $30,000,000+

Educational Requirements
While no formal education is required, athletes should be aware that they need some education to fall back on if they do not have success in the pros or when it comes time to retire after a successful playing career.

Certification or Licensing
None available

Employment Outlook
About as fast as the average

High School Subjects
Business
Health
Physical education
Speech

Personal Interests
Entertaining/performing
Exercise/personal fitness
Sports
Travel

Eric Roller grasps the tennis ball in his left hand, feeling the familiar rough fuzz against his fingertips. He bounces the ball once and steps behind his base line, staring intently over the net at his target, the service box opposite him. He wipes his forehead against the sleeve of his T-shirt, trying to clear the sweat from his face, and trying to clear his head of all thoughts except making the serve good—his best ever. Then in a quick, fluid motion he stretches skyward, tossing the ball up, raising his racket and bringing it down fast and solid. The ball slams into the box, right on target.

"You're still tossing it too far over your left shoulder," his coach interrupts from the sidelines. "You're losing power. Now go ahead and try it again." Eric nods and reaches into the brimming ball bucket at his feet. One practice serve down and 499 to go.

WHAT DOES A PROFESSIONAL ATHLETE DO?

A *professional athlete* earns a living by competing in sports events, either as an individual or as a member of a team. In individual sports such as boxing, tennis, bowling, track, and golf, athletes compete against one another for prize money. In some of these sports, such as boxing and tennis, the competition is one on one. In others, such as golf, track, and bicycling, each athlete competes against several others simultaneously. The winner in individual sports is determined in a variety of ways. Golfers win by completing the course in the least number of strokes; runners, bicyclists, swimmers, and race car drivers seek to finish a race in less time than their competitors; boxers, gymnasts, divers, and figure skaters look to a panel of judges who determine a winner based on a point system.

Athletes who participate in team sports such as football, basketball, and baseball are considered employees of a team and earn a salary. Teams compete against one another and try to win the most games. Professional team athletes are specialists, usually playing only one position, or one type of position, on the team. These positions determine both the players' locations on the field or court during competition and the nature of their duties. In baseball, a player might play one of the outfield positions, cover a base, or be a pitcher or catcher. Basketball players work as guards, forwards, or centers, and soccer and hockey teams have forwards, centers, and goalkeepers, or goalies. Because they are experts at their positions and are trained to cope with a specific set of duties and circumstances, modern professional athletes rarely, if ever, move into new positions. For example, a profes-

sional baseball pitcher works only in that capacity and will not be asked—except in an emergency—to take the field as a first baseman or possibly as a pinch runner.

Football, hockey, and soccer positions are typically divided into defensive and offensive roles. Football teams, in fact, have entire defensive and offensive sides that are never on the field at the same time. A team whose defensive side wins the ball then sends in its offense to score while the defense returns to the bench. In hockey and soccer, defensemen and goalkeepers are defensive players while forwards and centers concentrate on the offense. Baseball (except for the designated hitter) and basketball players play both offense and defense.

Whether working as an individual or for a team, athletes strive to be the best at their sport that they can possibly be. In order to aim for this goal, they maintain strict training schedules to improve their fitness levels. The exact type of training employed varies depending upon the athlete's sport and position, but most athletes do a combination of strength, endurance, and agility training. During this training they might work out in a weight room, jog, sprint, or jump rope, or practice balance or pivoting techniques. Athletes often work with coaches and professional trainers who help keep them motivated through drills, instruct them on improving their techniques, and adjust the difficulty and duration of the drills as the athletes' skills and abilities increase.

In addition to fitness training, professional athletes also spend many hours practicing their sport. For team athletes this means participating in scrimmages to practice specific plays and gain experience at their position prior to entering a real competition. Athletes in individual sports also try to simulate an actual competition, but the ways they go about this might vary. Tennis players seek out practice partners against whom they can hone their skills, runners and swimmers may race against a clock, and golfers play round after round in an attempt to lower their scores. Athletes also use practice time to keep themselves mentally prepared for competition, training themselves on how to perform well under pressure.

Many professional athletes earn a large percentage of their income through product endorsements, whereby the athletes agree to allow a company to use their names and picture in exchange for money. Endorsements usually necessitate that an athlete spend time at photo shoots, commercial tapings, and other public appearances. Athletes may also spend time speaking with the media.

WHAT IS IT LIKE TO BE A PROFESSIONAL ATHLETE?

"I got up around five o'clock every morning," says Eric Roller, a former professional tennis player who competed primarily on the Florida circuit.

"I'd stretch and then do a half hour of cardiovascular training, maybe running or jumping rope, and another half hour of interval training such as sprints or line touches on the court. After all that, the rest of my morning was dedicated to one particular shot I was having trouble with. Most of the time it was my serve."

Eric hit 1,000 practice serves a day—500 in the morning and 500 at night. How long does it take to serve 500 balls while being interrupted by instructions from your coach? About two hours. Next, Eric's coach "fed" him balls that he had to return.

After a short midday break, Eric was back on the court, playing practice matches that his coach had arranged. He'd follow this practice with 500 more serves and then seek out opponents at Morley Field in Balboa Park, San Diego, for pickup matches. These athletes would practice against each other until well after dark. "We played these games for money," Eric says. "It added pressure."

Lingo to Learn

bench The reserve players on a team.

draft An organized system for dividing players up among professional sports teams.

free agent An athlete who is free to negotiate a contract with any team.

personal best A personal record for a specific athlete.

qualifying event A preliminary sports event held to determine the athletes who will compete in the main event.

rookie A first-year professional player.

scrimmage A practice game played between two squads of the same team.

walk-on A player who tries out for and makes a team without being drafted.

Eric's rigorous training schedule is standard for the fiercely competitive world of professional sports. In order to succeed, athletes must be in the best possible physical shape and must have honed their skills to near-perfection. Athletes in other sports devote equal amounts of time to improving their skills, although the exact routines they perform may be different. Where Eric was picking up practice matches, a basketball player might be scrimmaging with the team and a swimmer might be racing the clock. Still, the intense schedule leaves little time for other pursuits. "I was ready to give everything to be a tennis player," Eric says.

Professional athletes perform when and where it is convenient for fans to watch. This means that their events are often held on evenings, weekends, and holidays. "It wasn't uncommon for me to play three or four matches in two different tournaments on one Saturday," Eric says. And because the fans don't travel to the events, the athletes have to travel to the fans. Eric traveled extensively throughout California, up and down the East Coast, and into the Midwest. Individual athletes tend to choose which competitions or tournaments they want to enter and then go to these events. For example, a professional runner may choose to enter the Boston Marathon and then travel to Atlanta for the Peachtree Road Race. Like Eric, professional tennis players are on a specific "circuit." Similar to a league for team sports, a circuit designates in which tournaments the athlete plays.

Athletes in team sports follow a schedule set for their team by the league or division governing their sport. Most teams play in their home stadium for a few days or weeks and then may spend several days or weeks on the road traveling to one or more cities to compete against other teams. Professional teams usually fly to "away" games, and the athletes spend significant amounts of time on airplanes, in airports, and at hotels. Because their schedules are tight, professional athletes usually go straight from the airport to the stadium or arena. Athletes who play for a team are essentially the "property" of that team and may be traded to play for another team in exchange for other players.

Professional athletes work both inside and outside depending on where their sport is played, and may train and perform under a variety of weather conditions. Professional football, for example, may be played in heavy snowfall and bitterly cold temperatures. Marathoners often compete in blazing heat or pouring rain. Because he couldn't let weather conditions affect his fitness level, Eric trained in all types of weather, though tournaments might be postponed in the case of extreme weather.

Athletes train year-round, and even those who participate in seasonal team sports must keep in good physical condition in the off-season in order to have their contract renewed and continue playing for their team. This means that athletes cannot take a vacation from exercising, ignore their diets, or stop maintaining their strength. Eric was conscious of his diet all the time, careful to maintain a healthy balance and eat only foods that

> ## To Be a Successful Professional Athlete, You Should . . .
>
> - have outstanding talent and ability in your sport
> - be highly disciplined
> - have strong powers of concentration
> - be self-confident
> - be fiercely tenacious in pursuing goals
> - be able to accept and learn from losing with the goal of turning it into a future success

would benefit his strength and performance.

Because their work is physically intense, professional athletes run the risk of exhaustion and injury. One serious injury can end a successful career forever.

DO I HAVE WHAT IT TAKES TO BE A PROFESSIONAL ATHLETE?

"If you want to be a pro, there's no halfway. There's no three-quarters way. Even when you're starting off and you're making a hundred dollars in your first round, you have to have desire," Eric says.

If you want to be a professional athlete you must be fully committed to succeeding. You must work almost nonstop to improve your conditioning and skills and not give up when you don't succeed as quickly or as easily as you had hoped. And even then, because the competition is so fierce, the goal of earning a living as a professional athlete is still difficult to reach. For this reason, professional athletes must not get discouraged easily. They must have the self-confidence and ambition to keep working and keep trying.

Professional athletes must also have a love for their sport that compels them to want to reach their fullest potential. Eric explains, "What I liked more than anything was the anticipation of going out there and hitting the shot I wanted to hit. If I'd been working on a particular shot in practice and it came up in a match and I made the shot I would get real satisfaction."

The downside of the profession, many athletes agree, is the relentless routine of training. While the fans see only the exciting action of the competition, events that may last just a few seconds or at most a couple hours, what they actually witness is the result of hours of repetitive training on the part of the athletes. "It was a grind," Eric says. "Every day the same thing. As a child, I played for fun. When I got older, we had a video camera at practice that picked my play apart."

Finally, Eric warns, you have to understand that sometimes you're going to lose. "If I lost a particular game in a match and it wasn't the one to lose, it would be astronomical for me, and I'd want to throw in the towel. You can't play that way," he says. "Being able to cope with losing is part of the equation for success."

HOW DO I BECOME A PROFESSIONAL ATHLETE?

Education

High School

Most professional athletes demonstrate tremendous skill and interest in their sport well before high school. Eric began playing tennis seriously at age 11, and says that this is actually somewhat late. High school offers student athletes the opportunity to gain experience in the field in a structured and competitive environment. Under the guidance of a coach, high school students can begin developing suitable training programs for themselves while learning about health, nutrition, and conditioning issues.

High school also offers the opportunity to experiment with a variety of sports and a variety of positions within a sport. Most junior varsity and some varsity high school teams allow players to try out different positions and begin to discover whether they have more of an aptitude for the defensive dives of a goalie or for the forwards' frontline action. High school coaches are there to help you expand upon your strengths and abilities and develop yourself more fully as an athlete. High school is also an excellent time to begin developing the concentration powers, leadership skills, and good sportsmanship necessary for success in the field. During most of his high school years, Eric participated in tournaments through the United States Tennis Association Junior Program.

Some individual sports, such as tennis and gymnastics, have professional competitors who are high school students. Eric, for example, turned pro at age 17. Teenagers in this situation often have private coaches with whom they practice both before and after school, and others, like Eric, are homeschooled as they travel to competitions. It is important for all high school athletes, whether competing on the high school or professional level, to remember that their first duty is to their academic classes. Most schools will not allow student athletes to participate in competition if their grades drop below a certain average.

People who hope to become professional athletes should take a full load of high school courses including four years of English, math, and science as well as health and physical education. A solid high school education will help ensure success in college (often the next step in becoming a professional athlete) and may help you earn a college athletic scholarship. A high school diploma will certainly give you something to fall back on if an injury, a change in career goals, or other circumstances prevent you from earning a living as an athlete.

Postsecondary Training

College is important for future professional athletes for several reasons. It provides the opportunity to gain skill and strength in your sport before you try to succeed in the pros, and it also offers you the chance of being observed by professional scouts.

Perhaps most importantly, however, a college education arms you with a valuable degree that you can use if you do not earn a living as a professional athlete or after your performance career ends. College athletes major in everything from communications to premed, and they enjoy careers as coaches, broadcasters, teachers, doctors, actors, and businesspeople, to name a few. As with high school sports, college athletes must maintain certain academic standards in order to be permitted to compete in intercollegiate play.

Eric played college tennis at West Palm Beach Community College, where he was an All-American and beat the number one player in the nation. "I really recommend college," he says. "If you get a good coach and a good team, you can have a great experience. It's an excellent place to work on your game if you do have aspirations of becoming a professional."

Internships and Volunteeerships

If you are interested in pursuing a career in professional sports you should start participating in that sport as much and as early as possible. With some sports, an individual who is 15 may already be too old to realistically begin pursuing a pro-

fessional career. By playing the sport and by talking to coaches, trainers, and athletes in the field, you can ascertain whether you like the sport enough to make it a career, determine if you have enough talent, and gain new insight into the field. You can also contact professional organizations and associations for information on how to best prepare for a career in their sport. Sometimes there are specialized training programs available, and the best way to find out is to get in contact with the people whose job it is to promote the sport.

Labor Unions

Many professional athletes are members of a players association or union. These organizations are instrumental in negotiating conditions and contracts for the athletes as a group. The Major League Baseball Players Association, for example, was responsible for the conception and negotiation of the professional baseball strike of 1994. Professional football, baseball, hockey, and soccer have similar organizations to which the athletes in these sports belong.

WHO WILL HIRE ME?

Professional athletes are employed by private and public ownership groups throughout the United States and Canada. At the highest male professional level, there are 32 National Football League franchises, 30 Major League Baseball franchises, 30 National Basketball Association franchises, 30 National Hockey League franchises, and 13 Major League Soccer franchises. The Women's National Basketball Association has 14 franchises.

Unlike many careers, you don't receive a license or make an interview appointment to get a job in professional sports. Instead, professional athletes become employed though a variety of other channels. In individual sports, athletes begin earning a living at the professional level by moving up through the rankings and winning competitions. Often this is done on a point system, with each win worth a certain number of points.

After having success in junior tennis competition, Eric turned pro at age 17. This meant that he began playing in tournaments to earn small amounts of money, and, more importantly, to earn points toward his ranking so that he did not have to play qualifying rounds. For example, Wimbledon has two qualifying rounds and hundreds of people might play up to six matches just to get to the first round. A player with a high enough ranking avoids all this preliminary play. Golf, track, and many other individual sports follow a similar system of qualification.

Athletes who play team sports are often scouted and recruited or drafted from college teams into professional sports. Once a year professional football, soccer, hockey, and basketball teams can draft, or choose, eligible college athletes to join them. Professional baseball players are scouted from colleges, junior colleges, and even high schools and hired to play on minor-league teams while they gain experience to enter the majors. Some professional baseball players never reach the "Show," but remain in the minors and earn a living at this level for the duration of their careers.

Upon joining a team, athletes sign contracts. These stipulate the length of time the athlete is expected to remain with the team and the salary to be earned during this time.

Athletes who have difficulty earning a living in their field in the United States or Canada may find a lucrative career elsewhere. For example, baseball is extremely popular in Japan and there are numerous European professional basketball leagues.

WHERE CAN I GO FROM HERE?

Advancement for a professional athlete depends on the sport. At the professional, major-league level, team athletes strive to increase their salaries and their playing time. Rookie athletes may spend several games—or an entire season—on the bench before getting significant game experience. Others may be in the starting lineup the entire season. Individual athletes continue to enter events in order to win and work their way up in the rankings.

Some professional athletes tackle non-performance careers in sports after they retire. After leaving professional tennis, Eric taught tennis at the youth level through clinics, camps, and summer recreation programs. He is currently back in college earning his teaching certificate in order to teach and coach tennis at the high school level. Coaching is an option for former team athletes as well. The coaching ranks of most sports are loaded with former major- and minor-league players. For example, Dusty Baker, manager of the Chicago Cubs and National League Manager of the Year in 1997, is a former major-league baseball player.

Former athletes also become team administrators, scouts, and broadcasters. Football star Dick Butkus found a successful second career as a sports commentator, and Hank Aaron signed on with the administrative staff of the Atlanta Braves. Some athletes also go into the design and manufacturing of sports equipment and apparel. Many of today's best bicycles, for example, are designed and even built by former competitive cyclists.

WHAT ARE THE SALARY RANGES?

The U.S. Department of Labor reports that athletes had median annual earnings of $39,930 in 2005. Ten percent earned less than $14,330.

Salaries, prize monies, and commercial endorsements vary from sport to sport; a lot depends on the popularity of the sport and its ability to attract spectators, or on the sport's professional organization and its ability to drum up sponsors for competitions and prize money. Still other sports, like boxing, depend on the skill of the fight's promoters to create interest in the fight. An elite professional tennis player who wins Wimbledon, for example, usually earns more than a million dollars in a matter of several hours. Add to that the incredible sums a Wimbledon champion can make in endorsements and the tennis star can earn millions of dollars a year. This scenario is misleading, however; to begin with, top athletes usually cannot perform at such a level for very long, which is why a good accountant and investment counselor comes in handy. Secondly, for every top athlete who earns millions of dollars in a year, there are hundreds of professional athletes who earn less than $75,000. The stakes are incredibly high, the competition fierce.

Perhaps the only caveat to the financial success of an elite athlete is the individual's character or personality. An athlete with a bad temper or prone to unsportsmanlike behavior may still be able to set records or win games, but he or she won't necessarily be able to cash in on commercial endorsements. Advertisers are notoriously fickle about the spokespeople they choose to endorse products; some athletes have lost million-dollar accounts

> ### Related Jobs
>
> - acrobats
> - aquatic performers
> - athletic trainers
> - coaches
> - jockeys
> - jugglers
> - physical education teachers
> - rodeo performers
> - scouts
> - sports announcers
> - sports executives
> - sports officials
> - sports statisticians
> - sportswriters
> - stunt performers
> - umpires and referees

because of their bad behavior on and off the field of play.

Other options exist, thankfully, for professional athletes. Many go into some area of coaching, sports administration, management, or broadcasting. The professional athlete's unique insight and perspective can be a real asset in careers in these areas. Other athletes simultaneously pursue other interests, some completely unrelated to their sport, such as education, business, social welfare, or the arts. Many continue to stay involved with the sport they have loved since childhood, coaching young children or volunteering with local school teams.

WHAT IS THE JOB OUTLOOK?

Competition in professional sports is fierce. There are many good athletes in the world and relatively few jobs. Eric attributes success in the field to a combination of extraordinary talent, determination, and luck. Jobs open as players retire, quit, or become injured, or with the creation of a new team or league. However, the number of hopeful athletes greatly exceeds the openings. In recent years, competition has become strong at the college level, especially in men's basketball, where thousands of good high school players vie for a few spots on the best college teams.

However, the general public is more interested and involved in sports than ever before, and as long as sports continue to sell tickets there will be a need for professional athletes.

Sports Broadcasters

SUMMARY

Definition
Sports broadcasters cover sporting events for radio and TV news; they write, produce, and edit feature segments for broadcast. Some anchor newscasts, providing scores and highlights. Others announce games by describing, narrating, and commenting on sports events on radio and television.

Alternative Job Titles
Color commentators
Play-by-play announcers

Sports anchors
Sports announcers
Sportscasters
Sports commentators
Sports directors
Sports reporters

Salary Range
$4,000 to $40,000 to
$2,000,000

Educational Requirements
Bachelor's degree

Certification or Licensing
None available

Employment Outlook
More slowly than the average

High School Subjects
English (writing/literature)
Health
Journalism
Physical education
Speech

Personal Interests
Broadcasting
Current events
Exercise/personal fitness
Film and television
Sports
Writing

With three seconds left in the final quarter, the receiver charges down the field, a swarm of defenders in hot pursuit. Fifteen yards, 10 yards, 5 yards, touchdown! The crowd jumps to its feet. Screams and the thunder of stomping feet roar through the stadium. The Orange Bowl has just ended, and work is done for the coaches, officials, and television camera crews—but for the sportscaster, the workday is just kicking into high gear. He now has hours of videotape to pore over to decide which parts of the game he will feature on tonight's news. He puts a tape into deck 1, and the editing equipment clicks and whirls. As the tape scans in fast-forward, he suddenly sees what he's looking for—that spectacular interception just before halftime. He hits the pause button on the editing control panel, freezes the frame on his monitor, swivels his chair to the computer, and begins typing copy. "The biggest upset in Orange Bowl history?. . ."

A voice calls from outside the editing booth. "You're on in 10!"

The sportscaster glances at the clock and finishes typing, then swivels back to the monitor and editing controls, one eye on the clock.

Lingo to Learn

conferences In professional and college sports, the groups into which teams are divided. (e.g., the NFL is divided into National and American Conferences).

demo tape Short for demonstration tape. A tape you give to potential employers when you are job hunting that shows how you look and/or sound as a sports broadcaster.

division In college sports, groups of teams, with the first division consisting of the most competitive teams, and the third division the least competitive.

franchise Membership in a professional sports league.

hat trick In a soccer or hockey game, three goals scored by a single player.

leagues Alliances of sports teams organizing the competitions.

play-by-play A type of broadcasting in which an announcer describes the action of a sports event as it happens.

press box The place at a sports event where broadcasters sit and report on the action. It is usually high up in the stadium for a full view of the field.

stats Short for "statistics." Numbers that denote an athlete's record in the sport. For example, a player's batting average in baseball is a stat.

TelePrompTer A screen displaying rolling copy from which a television broadcaster reads prewritten material.

WHAT DOES A SPORTS BROADCASTER DO?

Sports broadcasters work in two main areas: announcing games live as they happen and reporting on sporting events and personalities for broadcast news and sports stations.

Sports broadcasters who work as announcers present sporting events to people via television and radio. Some sports broadcasters work live from the press box of a sporting event, announcing the game as it goes along. *Play-by-play announcers* work to keep up with action of the sport as it happens.

In addition to announcing the action of the game, these broadcasters also provide information about the competition such as the score, the number of balls, strikes, and outs in baseball, and the downs in football. Sports broadcasters who do play-by-play also announce statistics about the event, which include information about players' past performances, records, and other facts. For example, a sports broadcaster reporting on the New York City marathon will announce not only the action of the race, but also the fastest time in which the race has ever been won and how close the lead racers are to breaking that record.

Broadcasters who work live from sporting events also do radio and television interviews with athletes and coaches before and after the event, and may do halftime or postgame talk shows, summing up the action and interviewing sports commentators, retired players, or other experts. Surprisingly, much of the work of play-by-play broadcasters is done before the event begins.

In order to announce a game well, sports broadcasters must know everything they can about the sport, the teams, the players, and the coaches. To get this information, they go to practices to observe the players and to locker rooms to talk with athletes and coaches before games. They review the pages of player information and statistics provided by the team and read every newspaper and magazine sports article they can. Sports broadcasters must know who is injured, who is on a hot streak, and who has just been traded to another team. This information is vital for a good broadcast, not only to announce the game well, but also to fill in time during a sporting event's many time-outs and other delays.

While sports broadcasters who do play-by-play announcing at games might only do broadcasting for one sport or even for only one team, broadcasters who work at radio and television stations announce all types of sports, from Olympic figure skating, to professional tennis, to high school football. Obviously, this means that they can't attend every sporting event they cover to do live broadcasts. Instead, these broadcasters do most of their work in radio or television stations, listening to or watching tapes of games and deciding which parts to use on their broadcasts. They write stories to accompany the tapes,

summarizing the highlights of the events for the audience.

Some sports broadcasters on radio and cable television may broadcast stories as often as twice an hour; sports broadcasters on television news usually present their stories twice a night. Of course, sports broadcasters who work for radio and television stations do attend some sporting events and are often seen or heard doing brief live broadcasts from event sidelines. Some broadcasters who work for radio and television stations host their own sports shows or specials where they interview coaches and athletes or ask fans to call in with questions.

Sportscasters usually work in clean, well-lighted booths or sets in radio or television studios, or in special sound-proof media rooms at the sports facility that hosts sports events.

Sports announcers who are employed by sports teams travel with their teams when they compete in other cities. Sports broadcasters who work for radio and television stations travel around their town or city to cover sporting events. They may also occasionally cover sporting events in other cities or even in other countries. "I travel short and long distances," says Tom Ristow, weekend sports anchor/sports reporter at WLUK-TV FOX 11 in Green Bay, Wisconsin. "There are days I have to go across town to a University of Wisconsin–Green Bay basketball game. Last month, I had to go to Oshkosh [Wisconsin] to do an ice-fishing story. In the fall, I'll travel to other NFL cities to cover the Packers on the road."

WHAT IS IT LIKE TO BE A SPORTS BROADCASTER?

Lars Peterson is a sports anchor/reporter at NBC-affiliate KTUU-TV in Anchorage, Alaska. He has been a television sportscaster since 1999, but worked in radio sports and news beginning in 1997. "I grew up in a small town called Naselle, Washington," he says. "It's located at the mouth of the Columbia River and the Pacific Ocean. It's a fishing and logging community and virtually hasn't changed in 20 years. Because of that, I grew up without TV—and I listened to the radio instead. One thing I have always enjoyed is basketball, so I would listen to the Portland Trailblazers [professional basketball] games. Bill Schonely, the announcer for the Blazers, sounded like he was always having fun. I thought, 'I want to have a job where you get to watch basketball and talk with the team.' That happened when I was about 12 years old, and even though I'm in television now, I'm having fun!"

Lars works 1:00 P.M. to 11:00 P.M. Monday through Friday. "In television (sports especially) you will always work nights," he says. "When I come to work, I am either sent out on assignment by the sports director (or something I have set up) or I produce the 5:00 P.M. and 6:00 P.M. sports for the sports director. Usually it involves tracking down local stories. Whether it's talking with our local college teams or our minor-league hockey team, I gather a story for the 5:00 P.M., the 6:00 P.M., or the 10:00 P.M. sportscast." After the story has been shot and the interviews are gathered, Lars returns to the station, writes and edits the story, and reads the copy during the 10:00 P.M. newscast. "My main job is to anchor the 10 P.M.

To Be a Successful Sportscaster, You Should . . .

- be a rabid sports fan
- have confidence in your abilities and never give up when trying to break into the field
- be willing to work at all hours and on holidays and weekends
- be willing to travel
- have a thick skin since fans won't always agree with your opinions or ideas
- be able to speak and write clearly
- be quick and accurate with your descriptions of the game
- be able to paint a vivid picture of the competition, especially for radio audiences

sports, my second is to report for the 5 P.M. and 6 P.M. newscasts. We have photographers here in Anchorage, but I shoot my own video about half the time. I do all of my own editing and writing except when I'm on a road trip with our satellite truck. In this instance, I usually have a photographer who both shoots and edits the stories."

DO I HAVE WHAT IT TAKES TO BE A SPORTS BROADCASTER?

The basic requirement for a sports broadcaster is a love and enthusiasm for sports.

Most viewers and listeners of sports news have this enthusiasm and demand it from their sportscasters. These audience members also want someone who is personable and trustworthy and who can speak clearly and express him- or herself in plain language.

Being able to speak clearly is of primary importance if you want to become a sports broadcaster. This means that you should not mumble, speak too quickly, or have an accent that prevents people from understanding you. Fortunately, many of these speech problems can be overcome with practice and training. Sports broadcasters must also be good writers. They have to put together interesting stories to capture the audience's attention during the news, to ask compelling questions of athletes during an interview, or to put together an entertaining presentation for halftime or other breaks in play.

Time constraints and deadlines can create havoc and add stress to an already stressful job; often a sports broadcaster has to race back to the studio to make the final evening broadcast. Sportscasters who deliver commentary for radio or television broadcasts have the very stressful job of describing everything going on in a game as it happens. They can't take their eyes off the action, and this can be nerve-wracking and stressful. "I had the luxury of being part of live game broadcasts when I worked in Mobile, Alabama," says Tom Ristow. "I've also done that here in Green Bay for FOX 11 Packers Family Night. It's live, and there is no script. You have to describe and analyze the game as it happens. I find it to be very rewarding when it's done well."

HOW DO I BECOME A SPORTSCASTER?
Education
High School

If you want to be a sportscaster, you need to learn the basics of journalism. In addition to courses that will train you in newswriting and reporting, interviewing, editing, and photography, you should take English composition courses. Physical education courses that offer course instruction in addition to exercise can help you become more familiar with the sports and recreation industry. A health class can teach you about fitness.

Though you may only really be interested in football, baseball, or basketball, you must learn about all kinds of sports to become a sportscaster. Watch ESPN, tune in to your local sports news, and read the newspaper's sports page to get to know as much about as many different sports as you can. Go to work for your high school newspaper or radio station, and cover the local sporting events. You may even find part-time work with the sports department of your city newspaper, or with a radio or TV station. Your guidance counselor may be able to direct you to a local mentoring program that could introduce you to professional sports journalists, allowing you the opportunity to shadow a sportscaster for a day or two.

Postsecondary Training

In recent years, broadcast journalism professionals have been debating the value of journalism schools; some believe students should pursue degrees in history and political science for a broader education. Others still stress the importance of journalism school for students wanting careers in broadcasting. Many journalism schools are offering majors in sports journalism, and even graduate sports journalism programs.

College is a time to hone your writing and speaking skills and to stay involved in current events, especially in the world of sports. Many colleges have their own radio and television stations, and if you're interested in becoming a broadcaster, participation in these is a must. At these stations you can gain valuable experience that will help you get an internship and a job while you are learning the field of broadcasting. Also, because most of these stations are run by student volunteers who are also interested in exploring the field, you will be able to participate in many facets of broadcasting, from live events, to news, to editing, engineering, and camera or recording work.

Internships and Volunteerships

Many TV and radio stations have internship programs, along with summer job opportunities. Most of these internships are unpaid; the paid internships offer better training, but are very competitive. If you're in a broadcast journalism program, your advisers can connect you to available internships; recruiters from network and cable sports departments may even visit your school. You can write to the networks for information on their internship opportunities.

If your community has a public access cable station, this is an excellent resource. Public-access stations train community members on the use of video cameras and sound and editing equipment and then let you produce your own shows for broadcast on the public-access channel. Consider covering your school's sports events or interviewing school athletes and coaches on a weekly cable sports show. To find the public-access station in your area, look in the yellow pages under "cable" or contact your local cable company. Public libraries also often have information on public-access cable.

Pete Byrne, a sports anchor/reporter for KVLY-TV in Fargo, North Dakota, interned for a production company in South Bend, Indiana, where he learned how to operate a camera, shoot interviews, and edit tape. His second internship was at WHME-FM radio, where he provided the color commentary for Notre Dame baseball. Pete encourages aspiring sportscasters to pursue an internship to prepare for a career in the field. "If you can get course credit or get paid, great," he says. "Even if you cannot, you need to learn the business you intend to get into, and this is really the only way. Broadcasting is not like most fields of work, where you earn a degree, and then get a job based on what you accomplished in the classroom. You need experience to get hired. It's a nasty paradox of the business. That's where the internships come in handy. I learned more about what I do now in two semester-long internships than in the rest of my four years of college combined. That was my training for this career."

Harry Caray: Broadcasting Legend

Maybe you knew him by his oversized glasses and his phlegmy, fingernails-on-the-chalkboard voice, or his trademark home run delivery of "There's a drive! Way back! It might be! It could be! It is! Holy cow!" Maybe you remember his sometimes garbled delivery of a player's name ("Ryne Sandberg" = "Ryneberg"), or his skill at saying them backwards, or his care to mention a fan or a friend on the air. Maybe you remember his love of the game—so strong that he occasionally ruffled the feathers of overpaid athletes who weren't getting it done on the field—and his devotion to his fans, who fell in love with his sense of fun, honesty, and excitement for "his" team, be it the St. Louis Cardinals, the Oakland A's, the Chicago White Sox, or in his last years, the Chicago Cubs. On February 18, 1998, after 53 years of broadcasting, the world of baseball—and the world at large—lost a broadcasting giant, Harry Caray. Harry became an icon in his later years, but many forget that in his prime, he was one of the best sports broadcasters in our nation, who offered concise and insightful commentary, and yes, an everyman's view of the game, to baseball fans throughout the nation. His is a success story that anyone, especially aspiring sports broadcasters, can take to heart.

Here is a brief outline of Harry's life and broadcasting career.

Early Years: Harry Carabina is born in St. Louis on March 1, 1914. After high school, he sells gym equipment, but soon realizes that he longs to try a career at broadcasting.

1943: Harry gets his broadcasting "break" by confidently telling a radio station manager in St. Louis that he could announce the Cardinals' games better than the team's current broadcasters. He doesn't get the Cardinals job, but the station manager helps him land his first broadcasting job at a small station in Joliet, Illinois. He also changes his name from Carabina to Caray to make it more memorable for the fans.

1945–69: Harry first utters his famous "Holy Cow!" in 1945. His energetic and opinionated style attracts legions of fans in St. Louis.

1971–82: Harry wins the hearts of Chicago fans—and fills the seats in Comiskey Park—by occasionally broadcasting from the bleachers, mingling with the fans, and using a fishing net to snare foul balls hit near the broadcasting booth. It may surprise you how "Take Me Out to the Ball Game" became part of Harry's repertoire during these years. White Sox owner Bill Veeck heard Harry singing along with the song and decided to secret a microphone in the booth to capture Harry's warbling. Veeck played it over the public-address system and a tradition was born—Harry began to lead the crowd in song each game.

1982–1997: Harry moves across town to Wrigley Field, and his broadcasts on WGN radio and the WGN-TV superstation make him a national institution. He is honored with the Ford Frick Award at the Baseball Hall of Fame in Cooperstown, New York, in 1989, and

(continued on next page)

(continued from previous page)

in 1994 is inducted into the National Association of Broadcasters Hall of Fame.

1998: Harry passes away on February 18, 1998. More than 1,000 people packed Holy Name Cathedral in Chicago for Harry's funeral. It is fitting that Harry's funeral ended with a moving rendition of "Take Me Out to the Ballgame" played on the organ as the mass ended and the mourners filed out of the cathedral.

Today: Harry Caray's memory lives on in his namesake Chicago restaurant, which is loaded with Caray and other baseball memorabilia.

WHO WILL HIRE ME?

In order to apply for jobs as a sports broadcaster, you will need a good-quality demonstration tape (*demo tape* for short), videotape for television broadcasting or audiotape for radio. These tapes are equivalent to an actor's audition: they show prospective employers exactly how you look and/or sound on tape. You may make your tape at a professional studio or announce a game at home while you watch it on television. Just remember to make the tape look and sound professional.

Some sportscasters get their first paying jobs from the stations for which they intern. TV and radio stations often widely advertise open positions; check your local newspaper for local positions, or consult the Internet for many job listings.

Sports broadcasters who do play-by-play announcing get hired by networks, specific sports teams, and by university athletic departments. Some of these broadcasters are hired after having worked for television and radio stations, and others use their demo tapes to apply directly to the team, network, or school.

Broadcasting and Cable, an industry magazine, runs help-wanted listings for broadcasters, and many sports broadcasters find job openings this way. Some television and radio stations and networks have job lines that list current job openings in the field with instructions on how to apply, and several online Web sites also post job openings and employment-wanted ads in the broadcast field.

WHERE CAN I GO FROM HERE?

Broadcasters typically advance in the field by going from a small station in a small town to a larger station in a larger city, and then maybe on to a network such as NBC, FOX, or ESPN. Play-by-play announcers may start announcing for a high school or small college team and after gaining experience may move on to a larger university, to a professional team, or to a network. Broadcasters may also move back and forth between working for a station and working for a team or university.

Advancement Possibilities

General managers manage the operations of television and radio stations; they're involved in marketing, promotion, contracts, and public relations.

Sports talk show hosts oversee local or national broadcasts that focus on sports, a particular sport, or an individual team. These broadcasts often feature live guests and listener call-in segments.

Sports television and cable anchors report sports news on local and national telecasts.

Television and radio producers work behind the scenes of television and radio newscasts and programs. They write scripts, hire and supervise staff, and bring together the many different elements of production.

A few famous broadcasters never worked their way up in the broadcasting career at all, but rather started near the top as retired coaches, athletes, or experts in the sport. This is true of former football star Dick Butkus and former football coach John Madden.

Some sports broadcasters leave the area of on-air broadcasting altogether to get involved in other aspects of the profession. They might become writers, producers, or directors of sports specials or news shows, or find work as station, network, or team administrators or executives. Others might get involved in the more technical aspects of sports broadcasting, including sound engineering, camera work, and editing. Some sports broadcasters teach broadcasting in high schools, technical schools, or camps, or earn advanced degrees and become professors of broadcasting at colleges and universities.

WHAT ARE THE SALARY RANGES?

Salaries vary according to the size of the market and/or newsroom, and the sportscaster's experience. According to a salary survey conducted by the Radio-Television News Directors Association

Related Jobs

- actors
- broadcast meteorologists
- comedians
- disc jockeys
- news anchors
- public-address announcers
- public relations workers
- radio and television traffic reporters
- reporters
- show hosts and hostesses
- sportswriters
- television directors
- television producers

(RTNDA) and Ball State University, television sports anchors' salaries range from a low of $5,000 to a high of $400,000, with a median salary of $40,000. For radio sports anchors, salaries range from a low of $4,000 to a high of $100,000, with a median salary of $32,500. "A lot of people are looking for work in this field," says Tom Ristow, "so you have to be willing to work very hard for a modest salary when you first get started."

Doing play-by-play for a professional team pays more than broadcasting on a local radio or television station, and announcers like John Madden, who broadcast NFL games for a major network, tend to earn the most money, with the most famous earning upwards of $2,000,000 a year.

WHAT IS THE JOB OUTLOOK?

Sports are more popular today than ever, and as long as people continue to watch and listen to sports news and events, there will be a demand for sports broadcasters. However, the number of people who want to work in the career greatly outweighs the number of openings. This discrepancy may mean changes in the future of journalism education; expect programs to develop more well-rounded curricula intended to better prepare students for the workplace.

Sports Coaches

SUMMARY

Definition
Sports coaches instruct athletes in the fundamentals, techniques, and strategies of playing a sport.

Alternative Job Titles
Instructors
Managers

Salary Range
$13,000 to $25,000 to $2,000,000+

Educational Requirements
Some postsecondary training

Certification or Licensing
Required in certain positions

Employment Outlook
Faster than the average

High School Subjects
Health
Physical education
Speech

Personal Interests
Exercise/personal fitness
Psychology
Sports
Teaching

It was the bottom of the ninth inning. The team's star relief pitcher was losing his composure. After a bloop hit, a hit batter, and a questionable walk (both teams had been complaining about the home plate umpire the entire game), the bases were loaded with one out and the opposing team's best hitter on deck. The stadium buzzed with excitement. The pitcher looked down, kicking the dirt in frustration.

The manager coolly surveyed the scene from the dugout. His team still had the lead, but the decision he was about to make would mean the difference between his team advancing to the World Series or simply going home and watching it on

TV. He could bring in a new pitcher or stick with the guy who had played a key role in getting his team to the playoffs.

The manager made his decision even before he reached the top of the dugout steps to the field. He walked to the mound, where the pitcher and catcher were discussing how to pitch the next hitter. The manager joined the conversation, offered a few words of encouragement and a slap on the back, and walked calmly back to the dugout.

Play resumed, and eight fouled-off pitches later, the batter hit a mile-high popup that seemed to hang in the dark blue sky forever as the crowd went crazy. When the ball finally landed safely in the

Lingo to Learn

bench The reserve players on a team.

defense The players and strategies used to prevent the opponent from scoring or advancing.

endurance training Training to increase an athlete's stamina and energy reserves.

offense The players and strategies a team uses to advance or score against the opponent.

roster The official list of players on a team, usually including the positions played or events competed in.

standings An ordering of teams or athletes in relation to each other, based on a team's win-loss record or individual athletes' times, scores, or points.

strategy A careful plan or method for competing in a contest.

shortstop's glove, the game was over, and the manager and his team were heading to the World Series!

WHAT DO SPORTS COACHES DO?

The specific job requirements of sports coaches vary according to the type of sport and whom they teach. For example, the coach of a peewee hockey team in St. Paul, Minnesota, has different duties and concerns than the coach of the San Antonio Spurs, a professional basketball team, and both of these coaches have different focuses than a coach for the Indiana University tennis team. Nevertheless, all coaches are teachers. They must be very knowledgeable about rules and strategies for their respective sports, but without an effective teaching method that reinforces correct techniques and procedures, their students or players won't be able to access that valuable knowledge.

The differences between coaching a team sport (such as basketball) and an individual sport (such as track and field) become more evident at the actual contest. At a basketball game, the coach gives a pregame talk to prepare the team for the competition. The talk may focus on specific strategies, on information about opponents, and on roster changes. The pregame talk is also a time for coaches to offer the athletes the support and optimism necessary to encourage them to play their best. Once the game is under way, the basketball coach might discuss strategies with another coach, yell plays from the sidelines, or prep a player who is about to be sent in by letting the player know his or her specific duties. Coaches also call time-outs during games to confer with their players and to alter tactics.

At a track meet, however, much of the coach's instruction has been provided before the players reach the meet. At track meets, a coach watches his or her athletes' techniques and makes notes for work in future practice.

Many team sports have several coaches per team. Usually the team has a head coach and several assistant coaches who may or may not be responsible for one specific area of the team. For example, a football team has a head coach, assistant coaches, running back coaches, and offensive and defensive coordinators, among others. In professional baseball, the head coach is called a manager, and he is aided by pitching coaches, hitting coaches, and base coaches, to name a few. Coaches who work in individual sports such as tennis or golf may work one on one or with small groups of athletes.

In addition to working directly with the players, all coaches have administrative duties. Coaches in professional and college sports work with team owners or college athletic directors to hire or recruit players. Coaches in youth or high school sports, and even some college coaches, are responsible for scheduling games and tournaments and arranging transportation to and from the competitions.

Most coaches of high school and youth sports have other jobs, either as teachers or in some other profession. Many high school sports leagues require that coaches also work as teachers at the school.

Coaches at the college and professional level have similarly long hours, although they work full time as coaches and do not combine their duties with another career as high school coaches do. College and professional coaches spend time meeting with players, owners, or athletic directors, drafting or recruiting athletes, developing in-depth strategies, and running extensive practices and training sessions. These coaches may also spend a significant amount of time speaking with the media.

WHAT IS IT LIKE TO BE A SPORTS COACH?

The career of coaching offers many highs and lows. Games are won and lost on last-second plays. Long hours may be spent in practice without seeing much result on the playing field. Some players exceed expectations, while others, despite hard work by both coach and athlete, do not. "Coaching is very rewarding and, at times, provides great feelings of accomplishment," says John Venturi, a high school football and basketball coach for more than 25 years. "It can also be an emotional roller coaster with great disappointments."

A coach may work indoors, in a gym or health club, or outdoors, on a baseball field, football field, or perhaps at a swimming pool. Coaches who work outdoors must deal with extreme heat or cold, rain, snow, or other demanding weather conditions.

During the season when their teams compete, coaches can work 16 hours each day, five or six days each week. It's not unusual for coaches to work evenings or weekends since those are the times when their teams compete.

One significant drawback to this job is the lack of job security. Athletic teams, especially at the professional level, routinely fire coaches after losing seasons. Coaches also have to deal with fans who may express their displeasure when their team does not perform to expectations.

DO I HAVE WHAT IT TAKES TO BE A SPORTS COACH?

Coaches have to be experts in their sport. They must have complete knowledge of

To Be a Successful Sports Coach, You Should . . .

- have a deep interest in and knowledge of sports
- know how to communicate with athletes of different skill and maturity levels
- enjoy teaching others
- have an optimistic personality
- be disciplined and be able to instill discipline in your players
- think and work well under pressure

the rules and strategies of the game, so that they can creatively design effective plays and techniques for their athletes. But the requirements for this job do not end here. Good coaches are able to communicate their extensive knowledge to the athletes in a way that not only instructs the athletes, but also inspires them to perform to their fullest potential. Therefore, coaches are also teachers.

Coaches must be disciplined and be able to instill discipline in their players. Discipline is important for athletes, as they must practice plays and techniques over and over again. Coaches who cannot demonstrate and encourage this type of discipline will have difficulty helping their athletes improve. Coaches must also be patient and be willing to allow their athletes to make mistakes during the learning process. Patience can make all the

difference between an effective coach and an unsuccessful one.

Coaches must be able to work under pressure, guiding teams through games and tournaments that carry great personal and possibly financial stakes for everyone involved.

John believes that two very important qualities for coaches are honesty and integrity. "Coaches also must be willing to work as hard or as long as necessary," he says, "and concentrate on the performance of their teams rather than results."

HOW DO I BECOME A SPORTS COACH?
Education
High School

If you have an interest in becoming a sports coach, you've probably already become involved in the field during high school by participating in sports. Maybe you're not an athlete but you're the sports editor for the school paper or you work as a manager for one of your school teams. All of these are excellent ways to develop your interest in sports, to learn about the skills that coaches must have, and to develop the leadership qualities necessary for the job.

You should also observe coaches and other role models to observe why they are successful. "Jot down positive coaching/teaching techniques utilized by your coaches/teachers," John advises. "Do the same for negative techniques. Do the same for five individuals whom you have observed, but who were not your teachers or coaches."

If you're interested in this field, you should pay special attention to physical education classes and to high school subjects such as health and anatomy and physiology.

Postsecondary Training

Postsecondary training in this field varies greatly. College and professional coaches often attended college as athletes, while others attended college and received their degrees without playing a sport.

If you are interested in becoming a high school coach, you will certainly need a college degree; in this role, you will most likely be teaching as well as coaching. At the high school level, coaches spend their days teaching everything from physical education to English to mathematics, so the college courses these coaches take vary greatly. Coaches of some youth league sports may not need a postsecondary degree, but they must have a solid understanding of their sport and of injury prevention.

In college, it is important to increase your knowledge of this field by volunteering as a coach's assistant or, if you're an athlete, by developing strong relationships with your coaches. Often, college and university student recreation centers train and hire students to work as weight room staff members who teach people how to use equipment, help them develop workout routines, and maintain and repair equipment. Students working in these centers also organize intramural sports leagues and teach classes such as aerobics or swimming.

Certification or Licensing

There is no single, mandatory certification for the broad field of sports coaching, but many workers in this field do need certification in specific areas. Since most high school coaches also work as teachers, people interested in this job should plan to obtain teacher certification in their state.

Internships and Volunteerships

It is possible to get involved in the field of coaching by volunteering as a manager for your school team, helping to coach youth sports, or working in a gym or recreation center. If you or your friends have younger siblings who play a sport, this can be a good place to start. Contact the team coach to see if you can attend a practice and lend a hand. Often, coaches of youth sports are happy to have good help, and high school students who assist in these positions may find themselves leading drills, refereeing a scrimmage, and even assisting at games. All of these are great ways to gain leadership skills and learn about the field.

You might also look into volunteering to help coach youth teams through Little League, American Youth Soccer Organization, or Pop Warner, or getting a job playing sports with children at a summer camp or after-school program.

WHO WILL HIRE ME?

Besides working in high schools, coaches are hired by colleges and universities, professional sports teams, individual athletes (such as tennis players), and by youth leagues, summer camps, and recreation centers. Methods for entering this broad career differ greatly.

Those interested in coaching at the college level must often be former college athletes who have gained significant coaching experience, perhaps at the high school or junior college level. Some colleges also offer positions for graduate assistant coaches, recently graduated players who are interested in becoming coaches. While receiving a stipend, these assistants profit from valuable coaching experience that they can put toward entering the job market.

No inexperienced coach will ever break directly into the world of coaching professional sports. Most professional coaches are hired after coaching successful college teams or after playing the sport professionally themselves. For example, Scott Skiles, head coach of the Chicago Bulls, was a respected professional basketball player before becoming a coach. Like athletes, coaches must gain a reputation for success over the years by offering positive win-loss records or, in the case of an individual sport such as figure skating, by demonstrating that their skaters become champions.

WHERE CAN I GO FROM HERE?

Because coaches are employed at so many levels of the sports industry, a coach who is interested in advancing to the pros can make a lifetime career of working toward it. In other words, there is a great deal of room for advancement within the job

title "coach" without ever changing careers.

A coach may even take years advancing within the coaching ranks of a specific team or sport. This is true for high school coaches up through the pros, where a coach might start out as an assistant, advance to coach of a specific area of the team, such as defensive line coach in football, and finally move up to head coach.

Most coaches never become head coach and instead find satisfying careers as pitching coaches, quarterback coaches, and assistant coaches. Also, many coaches advance by moving from one team to another. For example, an infield coach for one major-league baseball team could be hired by another team as manager. Some coaches move into sports administration and may become high school or college athletic directors or team general managers.

WHAT ARE THE SALARY RANGES?

Earnings for sports coaches vary considerably depending on the sport and the person or team being coached. The coach of a Wimbledon champion commands much more money per hour than the swimming instructor for the tadpole class at the municipal pool.

The U.S. Department of Labor reports that the median earnings for sports coaches were $25,930 in 2004. The lowest 10 percent earned less than $13,270, while the highest 10 percent earned more than $56,740. Sports instructors and coaches who worked at colleges and universities earned a median annual salary of $42,420 in 2004, while those employed by elementary and secondary schools earned $27,000.

Much of the work is part time, and part-time employees generally do not receive paid vacations, sick days, or health insurance. Instructors who teach group classes for beginners through park districts or at city recreation centers can expect to earn around $6 per hour. An hour-long individual lesson through a golf course or tennis club averages $75. Coaches for children's teams often work as volunteers.

Many sports instructors work in camps teaching swimming, archery, and sailing. These instructors generally earn between $1,000 and $2,500, plus room and board, for a summer session.

Full-time fitness instructors at gyms or health clubs can expect to earn between $16,000 and $37,000 per year. Instructors with many years of experience and a college degree have the highest earning potential.

Most coaches who work at the high school level or below also teach within the school district. Besides their teaching salary and coaching fee—either a flat rate or a percentage of their annual salary—school coaches receive a benefits package that includes paid vacations and health insurance.

College head football coaches generally earn between $150,000 and $300,000, although top coaches can earn as much as $2 million per year. Head coaches of men's college basketball teams earn between $150,000 and $250,000 annually,

Related Jobs

- athletic directors
- professional athletes
- sports agents
- sports executives
- sports scouts
- sportswriters and announcers
- teachers
- umpires and referees

while coaches of women's teams average considerably less at $100,000 a year. Many larger universities pay more. Coaches for professional teams often earn between $400,000 and $900,000. Some top coaches can command multimillion-dollar salaries. Many popular coaches augment their salaries with personal appearances and endorsements.

WHAT IS THE JOB OUTLOOK?

Americans' interest in health, physical fitness, and body image continues to send people to gyms and playing fields. This fitness boom has created strong employment opportunities for many people in sports-related occupations.

Health clubs, community centers, parks and recreational facilities, and private businesses now employ sports instructors who teach everything from tennis and golf to scuba diving.

According to the U.S. Department of Labor, this occupation will grow faster than the average through 2014. Job opportunities will be greatest in urban areas, where population is the densest. Health clubs, adult education programs, and private industry will require competent, dedicated instructors. Those with the most training, education, and experience will have the best chance for employment.

Coaching jobs at the high school or amateur level will be plentiful as long as the public continues its quest for a healthier and more active lifestyle. "If you are willing to work and learn as much as you can without concern for time and money, and love working with kids, then pursue this profession," John advises.

The creation of new professional leagues, as well as the expansion of current leagues, will open some new employment opportunities for professional coaches, but competition for these jobs will be very intense. There will also be openings as other coaches retire, or are terminated. However, there is very little job security in coaching, unless a coach can consistently produce a winning team.

Sports Executives

SUMMARY

Definition
Sports executives manage various departments for professional, collegiate, and minor-league sports teams. They also work for athletic associations and leagues.

Alternative Job Titles
Chief executive officers
Managers

Salary Range
$20,000 to $50,000 to $1,000,000+

Educational Requirements
Bachelor's degree

Certification or Licensing
None available

Employment Outlook
Faster than the average

High School Subjects
Business
Computer science
Mathematics
Physical education
Speech

Personal Interests
Business management
Selling/making a deal
Sports

Missy Bequette, director of basketball operations for the WNBA's Seattle Storm, says that one of her most rewarding experiences as a sports executive was when her team won the 2004 title. "It was awesome and tough," she recalls. "There were so many possible playoff scenarios that could happen, and having the logistics planned out in advance was critical.

"Over the course of the history of the Storm in the WNBA, it has been incredible to see and feel the fan and community support. Knowing how much time, planning, and effort has been put in by the many people in the various parts of our organization, this is a great WNBA atmosphere!"

WHAT DOES A SPORTS EXECUTIVE DO?

Sports executives manage various departments for professional, collegiate, and minor-league sports teams. They also work for athletic associations and leagues. They are responsible for the teams' finances, as well as overseeing the other departments within the organization, such as marketing, public relations, media relations, promotions/special events, accounting, ticket operations, advertising, sponsorship, and community relations. Sports executives also work on establishing long-term contacts and support within the communities where the teams play.

The two top positions in most sports organizations are *team president* and *general manager*. Depending on the size of the franchise, these two positions might be combined and held by one person.

Team presidents are the chief executive officers of the club. They are responsible for the overall financial success of the team. Presidents oversee several departments within the organization, including marketing, public relations, broadcasting, sales, advertising, ticket sales, community relations, and accounting. Since team presidents must develop strategies to encourage fans to attend games, it is good if they have some experience in public relations or marketing. Along with the public relations manager, team presidents create giveaway programs, such as cap days or poster nights.

Another one of the team president's responsibilities is encouraging community relations by courting season ticket holders, as well as those who purchase luxury box seats, known as skyboxes. Usually, this involves selling these seats to corporations.

General managers handle the daily business activities of the teams, such as hiring and firing, promoting, supervising scouting, making trades, and negotiating player contracts. All sports teams have general managers, and usually the main functions of the job are the same regardless of the professional level of the team. However, some general managers who work with minor-league teams might also deal with additional job duties, including managing the souvenir booths or organizing the ticket offices. The most

important asset the general manager brings to an organization is knowledge of business practices. The sport can be learned later.

WHAT IS IT LIKE TO BE A SPORTS EXECUTIVE?

Missy Bequette has been the director of basketball operations for the Seattle Storm, a women's professional basketball team, since 2001. She manages the operations of the basketball team on a daily basis, including planning for team and player travel, budgeting, overseeing the team calendar, coordinating logistics and information with other departments, overseeing equipment manager duties, and assisting coaching and support staff and players as needed. "In short," Missy says, "I do the things needed to allow the coaches to coach, the players to play, and the trainer and support staff to focus on their jobs."

Prior to working as director of basketball operations, Missy coached the Storm during its inaugural season, and also coached in the American Basketball League (Portland Power), at the college level (University of Missouri), and at the high school level (Southridge High School in Beaverton, Oregon). "I completed a master's degree in sports management," she says, "and knew that if I wasn't coaching basketball, I would want to be around sports/athletics in an administrative role. I have always been drawn to the business of sports, not as much in marketing and sponsorships, but more on the team side."

During the season, Missy arrives at the team's training facility between 6:30 and 8:00 A.M. She checks and returns e-mails and phone messages, prepares for the day and week (especially if traveling), works on a to-do list for the day, and manages any other tasks that need to be accomplished. "So much of the job," Missy says, "is just things that end up popping up that need attention, or giving information to those who need it. I work in our training facility, so the courts are right around the corner. I am usually at practice each day, which takes up two to three hours. I coordinate our scout team of male players, so I usually make sure we have enough guys to practice, as well." Missy leaves the office between 5:00 and 7:00 P.M., depending on what needs to get accomplished. On game days, she works longer—often not leaving until 10 P.M. She also travels with the team when it competes in other cities. "One thing that is important to know in the sports/entertainment industry," Missy says, "is that once you leave the office, your day might not be done, whether it is phone calls or work at home."

DO I HAVE WHAT IT TAKES TO BE A SPORTS EXECUTIVE?

Sports executives must create a positive image for their teams. In this age of extensive media coverage (including frequent public speaking engagements that are required of sports executives), excellent communication skills are a must. Sports executives need to be dynamic public speakers. "Building communication skills, whether verbal or written, is especially important," says Missy. "Strong interpersonal communication is vital in this type of position, because you work with a myriad of people—players, staff, outside vendors, people in the travel sector, etc. Being able to work with diverse personalities is something that at times gets overlooked."

Sports executives also need a keen business sense and an intimate knowledge of how to forge a good relationship with their communities. They also should have excellent organizational skills, be detail oriented, and be sound decision-makers. Missy adds that "being able to plan, to handle logistics of trips, to juggle a variety of responsibilities (multitask), and to look ahead to how things can be streamlined, to help not only yourself but also those you work with" are key skills for successful sports executives.

To Be a Successful Sports Executive, You Should . . .

- have excellent communication skills
- have a keen business sense
- have excellent organizational skills
- be detail oriented
- be a sound decision-maker
- have strong confidence in your abilities

Sports team management is a fickle industry. When a team is winning, everyone loves the general manager, team president, or other executives. When the team is losing, fans and the media often take out their frustrations on the team's executives. Sports executives must be able to handle that pressure. This industry is extremely competitive, and executives might find themselves without a job several times in their careers. Sports executives sleep, eat, and breathe their jobs, and definitely love the sports they manage.

HOW DO I BECOME A SPORTS EXECUTIVE?

Education

High School

High school courses that will help you to become a sports executive include business, mathematics, and computer science. English, speech, and physical education courses will also be beneficial. Managing a school club or other organization will give you a general idea of the responsibilities and demands that this career involves.

Postsecondary Training

To become a sports executive, you will need at least a bachelor's degree. Remember, even though this is a sport-related position, sports executives are expected to have the same backgrounds as corporate executives. Most have master's degrees in sports administration, and some have a master's in business administration.

Internships and Volunteerships

The majority of all sports executives begin their careers as interns. Interning offers the opportunity to gain recognition in an otherwise extremely competitive industry. Missy encourages young people to "build a network of great contacts in the fields that you want to be involved in and work on getting internships or jobs in that related field at an early age. I know that a lot of people in our company started out as interns, proved themselves valuable in those roles, and were hired full time."

Internships vary in length and generally include college credits. They are available in hundreds of sports categories and are offered by more than 90 percent of existing sports organizations. If you are serious about working in the sports industry, an internship is the most effective method of achieving your goals.

One way to start exploring this field is to volunteer to do something for your school's sports teams, charting statistics or taking on the duties of equipment manager, for example. This is a way to begin learning how athletic departments work. Talk to the general manager of your local minor league baseball club, and try to get a part-time job with the team during the summer. When you are in college, try to get an internship within the athletic department to supplement your course of study. Any way you can gain experience in any area of sports administration will be valuable to you in your career as a sports executive. You may also find it helpful to read publications such as *Sports Business Journal* (http://www. sportsbusinessjournal.com).

Sports Leagues on the Web

Ladies Professional Golf Association (LPGA)
http://www.lpga.com/default_rr.aspx

Major League Baseball (MLB)
http://mlb.com

Major League Soccer (MLS)
http://www.mlsnet.com/MLS/index.jsp

National Basketball Association (NBA)
http://www.nba.com

National Football League (NFL)
http://www.nfl.com

National Hockey League (NHL)
http://www.nhl.com

National Pro Fastpitch (NPF)
http://www.profastpitch.com

Professional Golfers' Association of America (PGA)
http://www.pga.com

United States Tennis Association (USTA)
http://www.usta.com

Women's National Basketball Association (WNBA)
http://www.wnba.com

WHO WILL HIRE ME?

Employers include professional, collegiate, and minor-league football, hockey, baseball, basketball, soccer, and other sports teams. They are located across the United States and throughout the world.

Entry-level positions in the sports industry are generally reserved for individuals with intern or volunteer experience. One you have obtained this experience, you are eligible for thousands of entry-level positions in hundreds of fields. Qualified entry-level employees are hard to find in any industry, so the experience you have gained through internships will prove invaluable in the early stages of your career.

WHERE CAN I GO FROM HERE?

The experience prerequisite to qualify for a management-level position is generally three to five years in a specific field within the sports industry. At this level, an applicant should have experience managing a small to medium-sized staff and possess specific skills, including marketing, public relations, broadcasting, sales, advertising, publications, sports medicine, licensing, and specific sport player development.

The minimum experience to qualify for an executive position is generally seven years. Executives with proven track records in the minors can be promoted to positions in the majors. Professional sports team executives might receive promotions in the form of job offers from more prestigious teams.

WHAT ARE THE SALARY RANGES?

General managers, team presidents, and other sports executives earn salaries that range from $20,000 to $50,000 per year in the minor leagues to more than $1 million in the majors. Most sports executives are eligible for typical fringe benefits including medical and dental insurance,

> ### Related Jobs
>
> - athletic directors
> - business managers
> - office administrators
> - sports association executives
> - sports facility managers
> - sports league executives
> - sports publicists
> - stadium managers

paid sick and vacation time, and access to retirement savings plans.

WHAT IS THE JOB OUTLOOK?

The U.S. Department of Labor predicts that employment in arts, entertainment, and recreation services (a category that includes sports-related careers) will grow by about 25 percent through 2014—or faster than the average for all industries. Although there are more sports executive positions available due to league expansion and the creation of new leagues, such as the Women's National Basketball Association, there still remain only a finite number of positions, and the competition for these jobs is very fierce.

Sports Physicians and Surgeons

SUMMARY

Definition
Sports physicians and surgeons provide medical care for athletes, people who work with athletes, and people with sports-related injuries.

Alternative Job Titles
Sports medicine doctors
Sports orthopedists

Salary Range
$50,000 to $136,000 to $250,000+

Educational Requirements
Medical degree

Certification or Licensing
Required

Employment Outlook
Faster than the average

High School Subjects
Anatomy and physiology
Biology
Chemistry
Health
Physical education

Personal Interests
Exercise/personal fitness
Helping people: emotionally
Helping people: physical health/medicine
Sports

Dr. Champ Baker Jr. says that one of the most interesting aspects of working in sports medicine is the diversity of his patients. "At one time," he recalls, "I was taking care of a Division I university football team, which was playing a game on national TV. One of the players went down with a neck injury. Play on the field was held up for 30 minutes while I went to the field with the trainer, made the assessment, brought out the spine board, stabilized the neck, and put the patient on the board and carried him off the field. Luckily, he regained feeling very quickly. He had no permanent problems and was able to participate four to six weeks later. The game then continued. But, because of the injury, we held up the game, held up the TV audience, as millions watched. . . . I had two physicians with me and several trainers on the field.

"The next week, I took care of my local high school team. On the last play of the game, a runner attempted to score a touchdown. He was unsuccessful, the game ended, players left the field, families started leaving, and, as I looked at the field, there was still one player left who did not get up. I went to the field. The player said that he did not have any feeling in his arms. The

EMS workers had already left the field. So, in contrast to the week before when several personnel took care of a player, I waited alone on the field protecting this young player until the EMS workers could be brought back, and he could be stabilized on the board and taken to the hospital. Fortunately, the young man had no permanent problems, but it underscores the need for an appreciation of the situation you are in and an understanding of your responsibility as a team physician.

"The contrast in coverage is enormous, but the problem basically remains the same: that is, an athlete who is hurt on the field needs your attention and expertise to minimize his injury and to ultimately help return him to competition."

WHAT DO SPORTS PHYSICIANS AND SURGEONS DO?

Sports physicians and surgeons provide medical care for athletes. They may also treat nonathletes who suffer athletic-style injuries such as strains and sprains, and nonathletes who are affiliated with sports, such as coaches, trainers, and managers.

Most sports physicians and surgeons work either for professional or college sports teams or for sports medicine clinics. Team physicians and surgeons concentrate on all of the medical needs of the athletes, and, in many cases, on the medical needs of the coaches and others who are affiliated with the team, as well. This means that they focus not only on athletic injuries but also on the colds and other illnesses of their patients. Sports physi-

cians also concern themselves with the psychological state of the athletes, who typically work under high-pressure, high-stress conditions.

Many team physicians have a private practice. This means that besides working for the team, they also have their own office somewhere in town where they see other patients.

Physicians and surgeons who work in sports medicine clinics focus on sports-related injuries, primarily musculoskeletal in nature, including strains, sprains, fractures, and joint problems. These doctors treat a combination of professional and amateur athletes, as well as nonathletes who need the help of doctors specializing in these types of injuries. (Think of your out-of-shape neighbor who strains every muscle in his back trying to move a sofa.)

Whereas sports physicians see patients in an office, diagnosing, treating, and preventing illnesses and injuries, sports surgeons spend a great deal of their time in hospitals performing surgery. Most sports surgeons are orthopedists who specialize in sports injuries, and they perform a variety of operations on the skeletal system. These might include surgically repairing badly broken bones, worn joints, torn ligaments, and ruptured discs, among others. During surgery, sports surgeons work with a surgical team including other doctors, an anesthesiologist, and nurses. However, sports surgeons also see patients in their offices prior to surgery to determine whether or not surgery is necessary or to explain an operation to a patient, and after surgery to follow up on recovery. Often, sports surgeons may decide that surgery is not necessary and instead prescribe other treatments, just as a sports physician would do. Some team physicians are also surgeons.

Besides treating illnesses and injuries, sports physicians and surgeons work in prevention, keeping in mind the importance of the future health and well-being of the athletes. They understand the specific conditions, rules, and risks of their athletes' sports and examine the players for any sign that they may not be fit for competition. They maintain complete records of the medical histories and concerns of all patients in order to best care for each athlete's needs. They may also work in conjunction with athletic trainers to help devise appropriate fitness programs for the athletes and to monitor past injuries.

Sports physicians and surgeons are responsible for explaining injuries, illnesses, and prognoses to coaches and managers and for making sure that the coaches are not requiring drills or other maneuvers that could compromise the physical well-being of an athlete. They inform coaches when players are not fit to play and make the final decision about when a player may return to practice and competition.

Sports physicians who work for teams attend practices and games. Here they work closely with athletic trainers to remove injured or ill athletes from play and to diagnose and treat them. Some injuries, such as scrapes and cuts, may be treated on the spot, while others may require a trip to the office or clinic for

---

Lingo to Learn

arthrography A diagnostic tool in which the physician injects a dye into an injured joint, which then reveals in an X-ray the exact site and extent of the injury.

arthroplasty An operation used to treat ligament injuries around joints. It can also be used to create new joints from plastic or metal materials.

arthroscopy A diagnostic or surgical tool. As a diagnostic tool, a tiny camera is inserted into the injured area to reveal the extent of the damage. As a surgical tool, it is used to remove torn cartilage or bone fragments from an injured joint.

computerized tomography A computerized diagnostic tool that combines X-ray images of the injured joint to create a detailed view of the injured area.

Magnetic Resonance Imaging (MRI) A computerized diagnostic tool that measures the effects of a magnetic field on an injured area to determine the status of the injury.

musculoskeletal Having to do with the muscles and skeleton.

residency The period of specialty training that is required after medical school and before becoming certified to practice medicine.

sprain An injury to the ligament.

strain An injury to the muscle and tendon.

X-rays or other treatments. In the case of a serious injury, team physicians determine whether or not to send an athlete to the hospital.

Sports physicians may also examine the sports facilities and equipment prior to an event and meet with sports governing bodies and event organizers to ensure the athletes' safety during the event.

WHAT IS IT LIKE TO BE A SPORTS PHYSICIAN OR SURGEON?

Dr. Champ Baker Jr. has been a board-certified orthopedic surgeon since 1978. He currently works at The Hughston Orthopaedic Clinic in Columbus, Georgia. He is also the president of the American Orthopaedic Society for Sports Medicine. "The most rewarding aspect of my career," he says, "involves helping a patient, be it an athlete or a workers' comp patient, or just someone who has a problem, get back to their pre-injury status—particularly, if the person has had a rather severe injury and/or if he or she has had difficulty for a long time. It is quite rewarding to effect a change in someone's life.

"My particular interest is sports medicine, and I specialize in arthroscopic surgery, in which small incisions are made, instruments are placed into the joint with a light source to look inside, and then another hole is made, and by watching on the camera inside the joint, I can manipulate, remove, and/or repair tissues."

Each Monday, Wednesday, and Thursday, Dr. Baker sees patients in his office beginning at 9 A.M. Over the course of his workday, he treats 50 to 60 patients. "My main job duty, as an orthopedic surgeon," he explains, "is to assess patients as they come into the clinic, try to make a diagnosis, after history and examination, as to what their particular problem is and then affect a treatment plan, whether it be therapy, injection, medications, and/or ultimately surgery. I also make rounds, if needed, at the hospital and go over dictation and answer workers' comp and lawyers' inquiries as they may arise regarding patient care."

On Tuesday and Friday, Dr. Baker is in the operating theater. "On operating days," he says, "the first patient's surgery begins at 7:30 A.M. and, depending on the number of cases, the day may run as late as 4 or 5 in the afternoon."

As part of his job, Dr. Baker travels one day a week to an outlying clinic. He is also active as a speaker at numerous medical meetings and travels to participate in these meetings.

Dr. Bill Grana has been an orthopedic surgeon for 31 years. He has been the head of the Department of Orthopaedic Surgery in the College of Medicine at the University of Arizona in Tucson, Arizona, since May 2000. He is also the past-president of the American Orthopaedic Society for Sports Medicine. "When I was in medical school," he recalls, "I decided I wanted to be a surgeon. I felt that the rewards of operative intervention and treatment of patient problems was much greater than the medical side of things.

"My current professional life involves administrative work as the head of the Department of Orthopaedic Surgery and clinical work, because that is how we support our department, and it allows the College of Medicine to have a Department of Orthopaedic Surgery. The state of Arizona gives us less than 4 percent of our budget. Therefore, we are really in private practice, but in a setting in which many of the dollars we earn go to the university, the College of Medicine, and the practice plan in which we work."

On Mondays, Dr. Grana's day involves primarily administrative activities that include regular meetings about the business aspect of his practice, as well as meetings that relate to his administrative responsibilities as chief of the orthopedic service at University Medical Center. "On my surgical days," he explains, "when I go to the operating room, I change clothes and put my scrubs on and then see my first patient. Then I go and check that we have the appropriate equipment and that the operating room is ready for the operations we are to do that day. On my clinic days, I arrive at the clinic, check the schedule, and assess patients who will require more time or who are having problems."

Dr. Grana also travels one day per month to an off-site clinic in Sierra Vista, a small town south of Tucson, Arizona. "[Work at] this clinic is particularly rewarding because there is a need for an orthopedic surgeon there," he says, "and the patients are willing to come to Tucson for their surgeries. Typical hours are 6:30 A.M. until 6:30 or 7:00 P.M."

DO I HAVE WHAT IT TAKES TO BE A SPORTS PHYSICIAN OR SURGEON?

"The most personal and professional qualities for orthopedic surgeons," says Dr. Baker, "obviously have to do with an affinity for helping and working with people. Above all, you provide a service and must be comfortable and eager to intermingle with the public. Professional qualities include dedication and willingness to endure some hardship to complete your training. For an orthopedic surgeon, the surgical skills are quite varied—anything from operating under a microscope to repair a nerve to doing a total joint replacement and using a hammer and power tools."

Sports physicians and surgeons often work under a great deal of pressure. They are responsible for the immediate care of injuries that occur during competition. This means they must think quickly and

To Be a Successful Sports Physician or Surgeon, You Should . . .

- be able to adapt easily to a variety of situations

- be patient and understanding

- be able to think and react quickly in medical emergencies and high-pressure situations

- believe in yourself and in your judgments and opinions

- work well with a wide variety of people

- be willing to travel with a team, if necessary

clearly, making swift decisions about treating the athlete. For example, sports physicians and surgeons decide how and when to move an athlete who is unable to get up from the field or court. They may also find themselves under pressure from coaches, team owners, fans, or the athletes themselves to get athletes back in competition as soon as possible. For this reason, sports physicians and surgeons must believe in their own judgment and be able to convey clearly both the facts and their professional opinions to coaches, athletes, and managers.

Sports physicians and surgeons must be patient and attentive in working with athletes, giving each athlete equal concern and regard. Because of the many patients, coaches, athletic trainers, and others whom sports physicians and surgeons see on a daily basis, they must enjoy working with people.

Sports physicians and surgeons who work for teams should be able to tolerate extensive travel well. They need to be flexible, because sometimes schedules change or things come up and they have to put their own plans on hold.

Sports physicians and surgeons must also be willing to continue to learn throughout their careers. "Orthopedic surgeons," says Dr. Grana, "must be dedicated enough to the specialty that they maintain a knowledge base that changes as time goes on. Orthopedics has changed dramatically in the last 30 years, and will certainly change again in the next 30 years. In order to be the best possible physician, you must keep up to date. I see so many physicians who do not keep up

and who still practice the way they were taught 10, 15, or 20 years ago. Continuing education is extremely important for an orthopedic surgeon."

Finally, being a sports physician or surgeon means you must find a way to cope with the severe injuries, illnesses, or even deaths of your patients.

HOW DO I BECOME A SPORTS PHYSICIAN OR SURGEON?

Education

High School

If you're in high school and interested in becoming a sports physician, you should take a full academic course load including four years of physical science, mathematics, and English. If your school offers college preparation or advanced-placement courses, these are a good choice, as they will help prepare you for the academic demands of college and medical school. Dr. Grana offers the following advice to high school students: "Students should get good grades in high school in order to get accepted to the best possible undergraduate school they can, focus on an undergraduate education in science, and then do the very best job they can in medical school to get a broad knowledge base they can use to get themselves into an orthopedic residency. Orthopedic residencies are among the most competitive among residency programs. If you cannot score within the 90th percentile on the standardized test, the chances are you will not get into an orthopedic residency."

In addition to a core curriculum, you should pay special attention to computer science, health, and anatomy and physiology courses. Physical education classes will help you learn the types of training required by athletes and also the demands that various sports make on the body.

By your junior year in high school you should be looking for colleges that offer strong programs in the sciences, such as biology and chemistry or premedicine. Your teachers or guidance counselors can help you obtain information from colleges and universities. Most colleges and universities have Web sites where students can learn about everything from campus layout, to tuition and fees, to laboratory facilities.

Postsecondary Training

In college, you will want to continue taking a full academic schedule of classes with a focus on English, biology, chemistry, mathematics, and other sciences. Psychology courses are important for understanding mental and emotional development, thought processes, and emotional and psychological disorders.

Because computers and technology play an increasingly important role in the sciences, college is a good time to continue your education in this field as well. Medical students commonly major in biology or chemistry in their undergraduate years, and others pursue premedical degrees. It is important for people interested in becoming sports physicians or surgeons to earn the best grades they can while in college. Medical schools are highly competitive and only the very best candidates are accepted.

Once you have earned your undergraduate degree, you must take the Medical College Admission Test (MCAT), the standardized test required for applying to medical school. Medical school lasts for four years; the first two years are centered on classroom lectures and laboratories. During the second two years of medical school, students begin to get clinical, hands-on practice, rotating through various fields of medicine and observing doctors as they work with patients. All four years of medical school are academically strenuous, with extensive memorization, test taking, and long hours.

After completing four years of medical school, students receive their M.D. (doctor of medicine), or D.O. (doctor of osteopathy). While M.D.s and D.O.s both prescribe medicine and perform surgeries, D.O.s focus on the importance of proper alignment of the musculoskeletal system.

Now that graduates have their M.D. or D.O. they're ready to practice sports medicine, right? Wrong. Now these former medical students begin one-year internships followed by residencies. Prior to beginning an internship and residency, doctors choose a specific field of medicine in which they want to specialize, such as pediatrics (children), ophthalmology (eyes), or neurosurgery (nervous-system structures such as the nerves, brain, or spinal cord). The internship and residency is the time to receive training in the specialty. Many sports physicians specialize in family practice. Besides family practice, the other common specialty for sports physicians, and especially for sports surgeons, is orthopedic surgery. Surgical residencies may last six or seven years. So, if you're interested in becoming a sports physician or surgeon you're looking at up to 15 more years of education and training after high school.

Certification or Licensing

Sports physicians and surgeons who actively practice medicine must be both certified and licensed. Certification acknowledges the completion of training in a specialty, and M.D.s and D.O.s take tests after completing their residencies in order to become certified specialists in their fields. While certification is available in 24 different specialties, sports medicine is currently not one of them (although subspecialty certificates are available for sports medicine in the areas of general medicine, family medicine, orthopedic surgery, pediatrics, and internal medicine). Certification must be renewed every few years, depending upon the specialty.

Licensure to practice medicine is granted by the state in which the physician or surgeon works. Each state's medical board determines the requirements for a license in that state, and licensure is required before a sports physician or surgeon can practice medicine in that state.

Internships and Volunteerships

As mentioned earlier, new M.D.s and D.O.s participate in one-year internships followed by residencies. As an undergraduate student, you will most likely partici-

pate in an internship that is arranged by your college. You might work in a hospital, nursing home, orthopedic clinic, or in another medical setting.

There are many opportunities for medical students—and people interested in becoming medical students, to volunteer in the field of medicine—though not necessarily in sports medicine. Frequently, charitable health clinics set up through churches, shelters, and other civic and human rights groups recruit volunteers to help with a variety of responsibilities. At these clinics, medical students might help prescreen patients, take medical histories, and administer shots or other medications. High school students volunteering at such a clinic might assist with paperwork, help entertain children in the waiting room, and observe doctors as they work with patients.

Dr. Baker suggests that high school students who are interested in becoming orthopedic surgeons should visit with and spend time with a professional in the field so they can see what a typical day entails. "There are many subspecialties within orthopedics that might interest someone," he says, "and students need to be familiar with the entire field in order to be able to choose a particular subspecialty that is special to them."

Another way to get a firsthand look at the field of sports medicine and injury prevention and treatment is to become a student trainer for one of your school sports teams. Talk to your school's coaching staff to find out about this possibility.

WHO WILL HIRE ME?

Sports physicians and surgeons are hired by individual professional teams, university athletic departments, and clinics that specialize in sports medicine. Many orthopedic surgeons are hired by the hospitals where they do their surgery and are considered staff members under contract to that hospital.

When applying for a position, sports physicians and surgeons must demonstrate their credentials by submitting a thorough résumé (often called a curriculum vitae), letters of recommendation, transcripts, and other information about their academic history and training. They also go through an extensive interview process, usually speaking with several other doctors, trainers, or staff members with whom they will be working.

Sports physicians and surgeons often learn about openings in their field through professional societies such as the American Orthopaedic Society for Sports Medicine and the American Medical Association. Professional publications such as the *American Journal of Sports Medicine*, *The American Medical News*, the *Archives of Internal Medicine*, and the *Archives of Family Medicine* are also excellent places for physicians and surgeons to find job opportunities. Many of these magazines offer online services, and job hunters may search ads through the World Wide Web.

Sports physicians and surgeons interested in working for hospitals and large clinics should also contact the human resources department of those institutions. These departments maintain job listings and may even have job lines or Web sites that include physician and surgeon positions. Some physicians and surgeons land their first jobs through contacts they make during their residencies or even in medical school.

Instead of applying to work for teams, schools, clinics, and hospitals that have job openings, some sports physicians and surgeons go into private practice. Essentially this means that they start their own businesses as doctors, buy or rent an office, and look for patients to be their "customers." After becoming certified and licensed in their state, family practice physicians and orthopedists with private practices can begin to establish themselves in sports medicine by introducing themselves to local high school, community college, and even college coaches in order to gain patients and build reputations. While it is expensive to start up your own practice, especially while you're building a reputation and signing on patients, private-practice medicine pays well and can be done in conjunction with work as a team physician.

WHERE CAN I GO FROM HERE?

After such lengthy training, physicians and surgeons begin their professional careers comparatively late and don't work their way up a career ladder from an entry-level position. Certainly some doctors make more money than others and have greater prestige, but this is usually a factor of years of experience and prominence in the field rather than traditional career advancement in the form of promotion.

Physicians and surgeons who work in clinics and hospitals may become *heads of staff*, *clinic or unit directors*, or *chiefs of surgery*. Besides practicing medicine, physicians in these jobs typically assume administrative duties such as supervising and hiring staff, making policy decisions, and representing the clinic or hospital to the community.

Some physicians and surgeons are also teachers, working in conjunction with teaching hospitals to train medical students both in the classroom and while seeing patients. Others go into medical research.

"I am toward the end of my career having practiced orthopedic surgery for 28 years," says Dr. Baker. "I plan to practice another 7 years and retire at the age of 67. At that time, I would give up the active practice of orthopedics, although I may still be involved in some teaching and/or educational programs."

Dr. Grana plans to retire in five to eight years. "I plan to continue to be involved in orthopedics, either on a national level, with involvement in continuing education courses, or on a local level, seeing patients in a clinic setting, but not operating anymore."

WHAT ARE THE SALARY RANGES?

The earnings of a sports physician vary depending upon his or her responsibilities

---

Related Jobs

- anesthesiologists
- athletic trainers
- dermatologists
- emergency medical technicians
- emergency room physicians
- kinesiologists
- neurological surgeons
- ophthalmologists
- oral surgeons
- pediatricians
- sports trainers

---

and the size and nature of the team. The private sports physician of a professional individual athlete, such as a figure skater or long distance runner, will most likely earn far less than the team physician for a professional football or basketball team, primarily because the earnings of the team are so much greater so the organization can afford to pay more for the physician's services. On the other hand, the team physician for the professional basketball team probably wouldn't have time for a private practice, although the sports physician for the figure skater or runner would, in all likelihood, also have a private practice or work for a sports health facility.

According to the U.S. Department of Labor, general practitioners and family practice physicians earned an annual net income of approximately $136,170 in 2004. Ten percent of these physicians earned less than $50,790 annually in that same year. Surgeons had mean annual earnings of $181,850 in 2004. These general figures do not include the fees and other income sports physicians and surgeons receive from the various athletic organizations for which they work. Again, these fees vary according to the size of the team, the location, and the level of the athletic organization (high school, college, or professional, being the most common). The income generated from these fees is far less than what these doctors earn in their private practices. On the other hand, those team physicians who are employed full time by a professional organization will likely make more than their nonprofessional sports counterparts, even as much as $1 million or more.

WHAT IS THE JOB OUTLOOK?

After years of watching athletes close down the bars after a game, coaches and management now realize the benefits of good health and nutrition. Within the world of professional sports, the word is out: proper nutrition, conditioning, and training prevent injuries to athletes, and preventing injuries is the key when those athletes are making their owners revenues in the billions of dollars. A top sports physician, then, is a worthwhile investment for any professional team. Thus, the outlook for sports physicians remains strong.

Even outside the realm of professional sports, amateur athletes require the skills and expertise of talented sports physicians to handle the aches and pains that come from pulling muscles and overtaxing aging knees. Athletes of all ages and abilities take their competitions seriously, and are as prone to injury as any pro athlete, if not more, because amateur athletes in general spend less time conditioning their bodies.

Sports Statisticians

SUMMARY

Definition
Manually and/or by using computers, sports statisticians compute and record the statistics relating to a particular sports event, game, or competition, and/or the accomplishments of a team or single athlete during competition. Others work for companies that provide statistics to television, radio, and cable stations and magazines and newspapers.

Alternative Job Titles
Official scorers
Official team scorers
Team scorers

Salary Range
$5,000 to $35,000 to $100,000

Educational Requirements
High school diploma

Certification or Licensing
None available

Employment Outlook
Faster than the average

High School Subjects
Computer science
English (writing/literature)
Mathematics

Personal Interests
Computers
Sports
Writing

"Sports is a worldwide, 24/7 venture," says Allan Spear, director of sports operations at STATS, a leading sports information and statistical analysis company. "And because sports data has a very short shelf life, everyone in this business is on call all the time. When there are problems at 2:00 in the morning, they need to be fixed right away. So while my job is 9 to 6, Monday through Friday, really, my job is every hour of the day, every day of the week."

But Allan says that there are definite pluses to working in the sports statistics field. "Because of STATS, I have been able to attend World Series games, All-Star games, Super Bowls, tons of baseball games, PGA events, and NASCAR races. This certainly helps balance out getting calls in the wee hours of the morning!"

WHAT DOES A SPORTS STATISTICIAN DO?

Sports statisticians compute and record the statistics relating to a particular sports event, game, or competition, and/or the accomplishments of a team or single athlete during competition. They use their own knowledge of basic math and algebraic formulas, alone or in combination with calculators and computers, to calculate the statistics related to a particular sport or athlete.

Statisticians work for professional athletic teams, television and radio stations and networks, private companies, and colleges and university sports programs. Often, they keep statistics for several teams at different levels of play.

Most high school, college, and professional team sports have an official scorer/ statistician who attends every home game and sits courtside, at what is called the scorer's table. The team scorer/statistician running stats at a basketball game, for example, keeps track of the score, the number of time-outs, and specific calls made by the referees, such as team and player fouls. The statistician is also referred to as the official scorer because if any item on the scoreboard is questioned—by a referee, one of the coaches, or another game official—the individual who ultimately has the power to determine the outcome is the statistician/official scorer.

Many statisticians still work by hand with a special notebook for recording the game statistics. As each play and call occurs in a basketball game, for example, the statistician records the play or call in a particular column or row of the stat book. Later, he or she makes a tally of the total number of player fouls, rebounds, assists, and field goals. These statistics, in conjunction with those from past games, can be used to determine the average number of rebounds in a quarter, for example. Many of these statistics might

not be used during the game itself, but they eventually become part of the team's history and are printed up in a media guide.

Statisticians use the same, predetermined algebraic formulas to compute the statistics for a single athlete or an entire team. Usually, the statistician keeps the stats for both the home team and the visiting team, including the stats of each individual player. At the end of the game, the statistician can then provide both coaches and teams with specific information on their respective play during the game.

Most professional athletic teams have both a manual scorer and one or more individuals keeping statistics with the league-sponsored statistics program. For example, both the National Basketball Association (NBA) and the National Football League (NFL) have computerized statistics programs that are used throughout the league or association. These programs, created by independent, private companies, allow each team to choose the statisticians who will run the system, while ensuring that the statistics systems used will be universal. One such company, SuperStats, created the computerized system for the NFL. In many cases, the computer system that calculates the different statistics also controls the different scoreboards in the arena or stadium, and can quickly and efficiently produce flash and quarter stats for the teams, coaching staff, and various members of the media.

In professional team sports, the home team is responsible for verifying that an

Lingo to Learn

box score The final, official game score.

error In baseball, a misplay by a defensive player that gives the team that is batting an advantage.

flash stats The stats distributed during a basketball game at every 60-second time-out.

stat crew The team of individuals who work to record and prepare statistics for the media and both the home and visiting teams.

time-outs A predetermined number of short breaks a team may elect to take in the course of a competition to discuss strategy.

official scorer/statistician is in attendance at all home games. The away or visiting team may have its own statistician or staff of statisticians, but the the home team hires the individual responsible for the official scores and this is usually the same person throughout an entire season.

Statisticians begin work by arriving at the arena or stadium in plenty of time to set up, greet the officials, peruse any announcements or press releases from the public relations offices of the home or visiting team, and get the starting lineups from both the home and visiting team coaches. Statisticians who work with computer equipment may arrive even earlier to set up their equipment and make sure the system is up and running well in advance of game time.

Once the game begins, statisticians quite literally cannot take their eyes off the game. They need to see every play as it happens in order to record it precisely in the stat book or computer. Often, the official team scorer or statistician keeps track of certain statistics, while other statisticians keep track of the remaining statistics. For example, the official team scorer for a professional basketball team is responsible for tracking the field goals attempted and the field goals made, the three-point shots attempted and made, the free throws attempted and made, the number of personal fouls, and the number of time-outs taken. He or she may record other statistics, but if there is a discrepancy it is these stats for which he or she is responsible during the game. A team of statisticians working the computers is responsible for taking down the number of rebounds, assists, steals, and so on. The most important aspect of the job is to remember that the statistician is doing more than compiling statistics; the statistician is recording the game, event by event.

Statisticians also work for television and radio stations and the sports information departments of colleges and universities. The jobs of these statisticians are nearly identical to that of the official team statistician for a professional team, in that they might record statistics in a manner similar to the one described above, but they might also be asked to do a lot of research and writing. Television stations often have a statistics and research staff responsible for collecting and verifying the statistics of any given sport. If the sport is fairly popular, they might assign someone to cover the events in that area, but if the sport is relatively young or not as popular, they might be asked to research information and statistics for that sport. The statistics and information are usually passed along to the sportscasters who are covering a game or event in that sport. Often, the statisticians are asked to write up notes for the sportscasters to use. For example, if the sportscasters are covering a baseball game, the statistician might come up with trivia or examples throughout the history of baseball when someone pitched no-hitters (a game where a pitcher does not allow an opposing team's batters to get a hit through nine innings or more of play) back to back.

Statisticians who work for private companies might be asked to keep statistics, field calls from sportswriters the day after a game about the stats for that game, or write up notes for one of their company's clients—notes regarding stats or trivia, for example.

Statisticians work both part time and full time, depending on the level of athletics in which they are involved, their degree of computer literacy and education, and whether they pursue freelance or full-time employment opportunities. The vast majority of individuals work part time, simply because they enjoy keeping stats for a team in a sport they love. Competition is incredibly fierce for full-time positions, whether for a sports information department at a college or university, a radio or television station or network sports show, or a private statistics company. Most statisticians advise students interested in entering the field to be persistent in asking for volunteer or part-time positions, to keep their schedules open in the event that someone calls with a chance to score a game, and to be realistic about the chances of finding full-time work.

WHAT IS IT LIKE TO BE A SPORTS STATISTICIAN?

Allan Spear is the director of sports operations at STATS, a leading sports information and statistical analysis company. He is also one of the official scorers for the Chicago Cubs and is on the stat crew for the Chicago Bulls. "I have always been interested in sports statistics and kept stats on a lot of games as a kid," he says. "When opportunities to work in the field presented themselves, I jumped quickly!"

STATS provides coverage of 37 different sports. "My department is responsible for ensuring that all of the data for these sports is accurate and databased correctly," Allan explains. "We have more than 30 people who are doing this 24/7, and I oversee this. Thus, my workday consists mostly of management, budgeting, and administration."

On a typical workday, Allan arrives at the office at 9:00 A.M. "I begin my day by reading operations reports from the previous night, then put out any small fires that may still be lingering. After that, most of my day is spent administering the department—dealing with budgets, doing long-and-short term planning, checking data veracity, and going to meetings. Very little of what I do is sports-industry specific. All the sports stuff is handled by my staff."

When the Cubs play a home game, Allan arrives at the ballpark about an hour before the game. Once the game begins, he makes all decisions regarding the statistics of the game. "I decide who the winning and losing pitchers are," he explains. "I decide if batted balls are hits or errors. I decide if runs are earned or unearned. And so forth. Now, 99 percent of that is spelled out explicitly in the rulebook, but several times a game you have to make a judgment on something, and your opinion then becomes fact. An example of such an instance would be if a batter hits a groundball up the middle, and the shortstop runs a long way to field the grounder, but when he gets there, he bobbles the ball and the batter is safe. Is this a hit or an error? That's a judgment call the official scorer (OS) has to make. The OS would factor in how far the fielder had to run to get to the ball, how hard the ball was hit, how fast the batter is, and if the ground caused any unnatural hops, and then make his decision."

Allan follows a similar pregame ritual when he works as a statistician for the Chicago Bulls. "Once the game begins," he says, "our crew of three watches what is happening on the court, then translates that into the statistics of the game. Again, pretty much everything is spelled out in the rulebook, but you have to make judgments in a lot of areas. An example of a basketball-related judgment call could occur when a player passes the ball to a cutting teammate, who makes a spin move before making a layup. Should the first player get an assist on the play? If the player who scored made his move in the context of the whole play, then probably. But if the player who scored stopped, then made his spin move, then probably no assist would be given out."

Statisticians routinely work in the same conditions as do others in professions related to sports coverage, such as sportscasters, sportswriters, and sports agents. That is, they may spend time outdoors, in pleasant and inclement weather, but they also spend a lot of time indoors, in the media and statistics areas of sports stadiums and arenas, and in their own offices.

Statisticians also work odd hours, including weekends and holidays. In short, whenever there is a sports event scheduled that requires scorekeeping and statistics, one or more statisticians will be covering it. This can wreak havoc on holidays, such as Christmas and the Fourth of July; some football and many basketball games are scheduled on Christmas Eve and Christmas Day, and there are

To Be a Successful Sports Statistician, You Should . . .

- be able to work well under pressure-filled game situations

- be mathematically adept and a stickler for details

- be willing to work odd hours, including weekends and holidays

- be willing to work outdoors in inclement weather

countless professional baseball games played on Independence Day.

DO I HAVE WHAT IT TAKES TO BE A SPORTS STATISTICIAN?

Allan believes that knowledge of sports is crucial to success in the field. "Understanding database design is pretty important, too," he adds. "But the most important thing is a sense of personal responsibility, a devotion to accuracy, and dependability. If you forget you have a game one day, a lot of people are negatively influenced."

Depending on the sport and the atmosphere of the game, the statistician's job can become pretty tense. In an instant, all the attention can focus on the statistician when a ref asks for a call on some aspect of the game. The pressure to be vigilant 100 percent of the time can be incredible.

HOW DO I BECOME A SPORTS STATISTICIAN?

Education

High School

Technically, there are no formal educational requirements for the job of sports statistician. Knowing how to manually score a game or event, and knowing as much as possible about the sport or sports for which you would like to keep statistics, are probably the only true requirements, but there are plenty of informal requirements that prospective sports statisticians should keep in mind. Knowledge of computer software and sports is key to being successful in the field of sports statistics.

First and foremost, although knowledge of manual scoring is essential, the future of sports statistics is tied to computers. The more you know about computers—from navigating your way around a keyboard to programming to troubleshooting—the better. Because most of the computer systems for the professional teams are privately owned and created expressly for the league or association, you won't actually be able to study the programs used by professional teams. Becoming computer literate and having a working knowledge of common computer systems and programs, however, is the best way to ensure that, if necessary, you can pick up the intricacies of a new program.

Secondly, having a solid grasp of basic math skills is a necessity. In order to compute home run averages, you need to be able to figure averages. The formulas used to arrive at the different statistics are fairly simple, but you must be good enough with math to figure them out yourself. On the job you will probably use a calculator or computer, but if the computer system goes out you need to be able to do the math.

Good writing and communication skills are also vital to the statistician; you may find yourself trying to explain a statistic to a sportscaster or writer, or you may be asked to write notes concerning relevant statistics or trivia, even a press release. If you can't communicate information quickly and intelligently, you might find yourself out of a job.

Postsecondary Training

Private companies that employ sports statisticians will most likely require candidates to have a bachelor's degree in a related field, such as marketing, accounting, communications, business administration, or sports administration. Allan has a Bachelor of Science in marketing from Pennsylvania State University and a master of business administration from Missouri State University. "While at Penn State, I spent my senior year working in the sports information department," he says. "When I went to Missouri State, I was a sports information graduate assistant. I was also a sports fan growing up, so between my childhood sports learning and my two college jobs, I was pretty prepared for the real sports world."

Internships and Volunteerships

If you attend college, you may be required to participate in an internship. This hands-on work experience at a company employing statisticians will allow give you a great introduction to the field and help you make contacts in the industry. Internships typically last 4 to 12 months and are usually arranged by the school, especially when the internship is a requirement for the degree. Although most internships are unpaid, many schools offer college credit for their completion.

Outside of formal educational opportunities, the best way to gain experience in this field is to learn as much as possible about how a sport is played, and how to score it, especially those sports you enjoy most. High school and college students can easily accomplish this by participat-ing in sports or volunteering to act as statistician for one of the teams. If neither of these options is possible, then you can begin to pick up the finer points of scoring by attending games as often as possible and scoring the various aspects of each game.

There are books available on nearly every sport that explain, in detail, how to correctly score particular statistics, but there is a better, more expedient way. Look around you at the next high school baseball or basketball game. Chances are a seasoned veteran of statistics is no less than two yards away. During a break or—better yet—after the game, introduce yourself and ask that person how to score a game; most statisticians learned how to score sports events in precisely this way—by asking the people who have been doing it for years.

Another good reason for getting to know the old-timers and professional scorers in this way is that one day they might need someone to cover a game, or know of an opening for a part-time statistician.

WHO WILL HIRE ME?

Luck, timing, and preparation all play a part in finding work in this competitive field. Many statisticians find part-time jobs while still in high school and continue these jobs through college. Others go on to score stats for various teams at their college or university. The sports information departments at colleges and universities are also good places to look for part-time work. You might be assigned to the public relations office, in which

(continued on page 88)

"Hey, Batter, Batter, Batter, Batter!"

Experts agree, the best way to learn sports statistics is to learn how to score a game. To do this, statisticians use abbreviations for the different aspects of the game, as well as for the different percentages. Knowing and using these abbreviations will make learning to score that much easier, not to mention how much more knowledgeable you will sound if you need to ask an old-timer for advice or information. We've collected some of the abbreviations and symbols needed to score a baseball game in terms of a batter's performance. Remember, though, there are also stats for pitchers and fielders, and for specific types of plays.

G = Games

AB = At-Bats

H = Hits

2B = Doubles

3B = Triples

HR = Home runs

Hm = Home runs at home

Rd = Home runs on the Road

TB = Total bases

R = Runs

RBI = Runs Batted In

TBB = Total Bases on Balls

IBB = Intentional Bases on Balls

SO = Strikeouts

HBP = Times Hit by Pitches

SH = Sacrifice Hits

SF = Sacrifice Flies

SB = Stolen Bases

CS = Times Caught Stealing

SB% = Stolen Base Percentage

GDP = Times Grounded into Double Plays

Avg = Batting Average

OBP = On-base Percentage

SLG = Slugging Percentage

BB = Walks

PA = Plate Appearances

RAT = Ratio of AB/HR

RC = Runs Created

RC/27 = Runs Created per 27 outs

Ht = Height

Wt = Weight

Yr = Year

Lg = Minor League Level

POS = Position

GB = Number of Fair Ground Balls Hit (hits, outs, and errors)

FB = Number of Fly Balls Hit (excludes line drives)

G/F = Ratio of Grounders to Fly Balls

BFP = Batters Facing Pitchers

#Pit = Number of Pitches Offered to the Hitter

#P/PA = Average Number of Pitches per Plate Appearance

* = Bats Left-handed

= Switch Hitter

case you would learn the related tasks—fielding calls from the media, writing press releases, and researching statistics for a specific team. Or, you might be assigned to work directly with a team as a statistician. In either case, many statisticians continue to volunteer or work part time at stats jobs in order to maintain their scoring skills.

Television and radio stations are yet another way into the field of sports statistics. As mentioned, contacts are very helpful, but you can also send your résumé to the sports departments of various stations and channels and ask if they need another statistician. Be ready to volunteer, if necessary, or to work in the sometimes humbling position of a gofer. One longtime statistician advises prospective statisticians to be ready to score any game, anytime, anywhere, because one never knows which contact will eventually lead to something bigger and better. This also means being prepared to sacrifice personal time to a last-minute request from a statistician to cover a game in an emergency when the regular person can't be there.

Finally, there are three major companies that work with sports statistics: ESPN/SportsTicker, Elias Sports Bureau, and STATS (where Allan is employed). These companies employ statisticians and researchers to help provide clients (television, radio, and cable stations; magazines and newspapers) with sports statistics and research on a daily basis. These companies often offer internships and part-time jobs and are definitely one avenue to pursue for full-time jobs.

WHERE CAN I GO FROM HERE?

Part-time jobs keeping statistics for high school and college and university athletic teams can often lead to stats jobs with other organizations, including radio and television stations and private organizations, like Elias Sports Bureau, ESPN/ SportsTicker, and STATS. While some people may leave these jobs to take others, most stay in them for many years.

Statisticians who build a solid reputation, know the ins and outs of a particular sport, and have excellent communication and writing skills can often advance in the field to work for large radio and television networks.

In the next decade, Allan hopes to continue working for the Cubs and the Bulls, as well as for STATS.

WHAT ARE THE SALARY RANGES?

On the whole, competition will be keen for full-time jobs that offer competitive salaries in sports statistics. It is important to realize that many statisticians must work full-time jobs, often in totally unrelated fields, in order to support themselves. Only their love of the sport and statistics—and not the financial rewards of the jobs—keeps them involved with sports statistics.

Even for part-timers, much depends on the level of athletics in which the statistician is involved. For example, a statistician working freelance for a radio station, and covering an expansion professional basketball team, might receive $35 per game, whereas a statistician working free-lance for one of the large television net-works, like FOX, might receive anywhere from $400 to $500 per game.

On the other hand, statisticians who work full time for radio and television, or for companies like Elias Sports Bureau, receive salaries competitive with jobs in other fields. An individual working with one of these companies for between one and five years might earn $25,000 to $35,000 a year. If that person stayed with the company for another five to 10 years, he or she might earn between $35,000 and $50,000 a year. Statisticians who work for a company for many years can earn anywhere between $75,000 and $100,000 a year. Again, competition for these posi-tions is extremely intense.

In comparison to statisticians who work in the more traditional fields of sta-tistical analysis, both in government and nongovernment jobs, sports statisticians with full-time positions have the oppor-tunity to earn considerably higher sala-ries, although this may not always be the case. According to the U.S. Department of Labor, the average annual salary for statisticians was $58,620 in 2004.

WHAT IS THE JOB OUTLOOK?

As the computer's role in statistics-gather-ing increases, fewer and fewer individuals will be able to make their careers solely as sports statisticians for professional sports teams, at least not in the capacity of some-one manually scoring the games. Accord-ing to experts in the field of sports statistics,

> ### Related Jobs
> • actuaries
> • computer programmers
> • demographers
> • economists
> • financial analysts
> • mathematical technicians
> • mathematicians
> • sociologists
> • systems analysts

while it's likely that someone will always be manually scoring the games, this job will most likely become a part-time job.

As the impact of cable television and satellite reception enhances the market-ability of the top five sports—baseball, basketball, football, hockey, and soccer—it will also bring into viewers' living rooms many sports not previously car-ried by the major networks. All of this increased sports coverage, plus develop-ing technologies and markets on the Internet, will only increase the demand for sports statistics and the individuals who record and catalog them. "People all across the world seem to love sports and sports statistics," Allan says. "As long as that holds true, I think the sports statis-tics industry will continue to grow and grow and grow."

It is important to remember the effect new technology will have on those seek-ing jobs in sports statistics, as computer skills will become just as valuable to those interested in a career in sports statistics as in-depth knowledge of a sport. Those individuals who do have computer skills will be increasingly marketable in the years to come. People already in the field will, perhaps, want to develop some degree of computer literacy.

On another note, even as the field develops, those currently in full-time positions in sports statistics aren't likely to leave those jobs. However, attrition rates due to retirement and advancement, combined with new jobs, should keep this field developing just slightly faster than the average.

Sportswriters

SUMMARY

Definition
Sportswriters cover the news in sports for newspapers and magazines.

Alternative Job Titles
Sports journalists

Salary Range
$23,000 to $45,000 to $87,000+

Educational Requirements
Bachelor's degree

Certification or Licensing
None available

Employment Outlook
About as fast as the average

High School Subjects
English

Journalism
Physical education

Personal Interests
Current events
Reading/books
Sports
Travel
Writing

Emyville High's basketball team was about to make history. Three seconds remained in the small-school state championship game, the score was 41-39 Emyville, and Emyville's star player was at the free throw line shooting the last of two foul shots.

The sportswriter sat near the team's bench, typing rapidly on her laptop computer. If Emyville, a team from a tiny town of 300 in the state's farm country, won, this would be the biggest upset in high school sports in her state in ages.

Swish. 42-39 Smithville. The crowd erupted, cheering and pounding their feet on the wooden bleachers.

Emyville's opponent inbounded the ball, but could not score as time expired.

Pandemonium erupted as the crowd cheered and rushed onto the court. But the sportswriter had no time to get caught up in the excitement. She was already weaving her way through the crowd toward the team's players and coach, tape recorder in hand, ready to get the scoop on how a team that wasn't expected to have a winning record had captured the state championship.

WHAT DOES A SPORTSWRITER DO?

The primary job of the *sportswriter* is to report the outcomes of the sports events that occurred that day. A sportswriter begins work each day by reviewing the local, national, and international news that comes in over the wire news services; reading local and national newspapers and magazines that cover sports; and watching sports on local television or national cable sports channels. He or she then begins researching the top or lead stories to try to flesh out the story, perhaps with a local perspective on it, or to come up with an altogether new angle. The writer may have also attended a sports competition the day before and use the notes and recorded interviews to help write the story. An example of a lead story might be the comeback of a professional tennis star; the underdog victory of a third-rate, much-maligned football team; the incredible pitching record of a high school athlete; or the details about a football running back who blew out his knee in a crucial last-minute play. The sportswriter then interviews coaches, athletes, scouts, agents, promoters, and sometimes, in the case of an athletic injury, a physician or team of physicians.

Depending on the edition of the newspaper or magazine, the sportswriter might report events that happened anywhere from the day before to events that took place within that week or month. For example, a sportswriter who writes for a magazine such as *Sports Illustrated* probably won't write articles with the same degree of detail per game. Instead, he or she writes articles, commonly called features, that explore an entire season for a team or an athlete. The *magazine sportswriter* might take the same story of the running back with the damaged knee lig-

aments and follow that athlete through his surgery and rehabilitation, interviewing not only the running back, but also his wife, doctors, coaches, and agent. This stage of gathering information is the same for both newspaper and magazine sportswriters, the only difference being the timeline; a newspaper sportswriter may have only a few hours to conduct research and call around for comments, while the sportswriter for a magazine may have anywhere from several weeks to several months to compose the story.

Regardless of whether the sportswriter works for a newspaper or magazine, the next step for the sportswriter is to write the story. The method will vary, again, depending on the medium. Most sportswriters for newspapers are subject to the constraints of space, and these limits can change in a matter of minutes. On a dull day, up until the hour before the paper is published, or put to bed, the sportswriter might have a quarter of a page to fill with local sports news. At the last minute, however, an entire Super Bowl team could come down with food poisoning, in which case the sports editor would want to cover this larger, breaking story. To accommodate the new articles about the poisoning—the effect on team morale and whether or not the Super Bowl might be postponed for the first time in history—the local sports coverage would either have to shrink considerably or be completely cut. To manage this, sportswriters, like other reporters who write for daily newspapers, compose their stories with the most crucial facts contained within the first one or two paragraphs of the story. They may write a 10-paragraph story, but if it had to be shortened, the pertinent information would be easily retained.

Sportswriters for magazines, on the other hand, seldom need to worry about their stories being cut down at the last minute. Rather, their stories are subject to more careful editing. Magazines usually have story meetings weeks or months in advance of the relevant issue, giving sportswriters ample time to plan, research, and write their articles. As a result of the different timetable, the presentation of the story will change. The sportswriter will not cram all the essential facts into an opening paragraph or two. Instead, he or she is allowed much greater leeway with the introduction and the rest of the article. The sportswriter, in this case, will want to set a mood in the introduction, developing the characters of the individuals being interviewed—literally, telling a story about the story. In short, details can hinder a newspaper sports story from accomplishing its goal of getting across the facts in a concise form, while in a magazine sports article, those extraneous, revealing details actually become part of the story.

Even with the help of news services, sportswriters still couldn't have all the sports news at their fingertips without the help of other reporters and writers, known in the world of reporting as *stringers*. A stringer covers an event that, most likely, would not be covered by the wire services—such as high school sports events or games in professional sports that are occurring simultaneously with other major sports events. The stringer attends the sports event and phones in scores, or e-mails or faxes in a complete report.

Whereas sportswriters for magazines don't necessarily specialize in one area of sports but, instead, routinely write features on a wide variety of sports and athletes, sportswriters for newspapers do specialize. Many only cover a particular sport, such as baseball. Others are assigned a beat, or specific area, and like other reporters must cover all the events that fall into that beat. For example, a sportswriter assigned to the high school football beat for a newspaper in Los Angeles, California, would be expected to cover all the area high school football games. Since football is seasonal, he or she might be assigned to the high school basketball beat during the winter season. On the other hand, the sportswriter working in Lexington, Kentucky, might be assigned coverage of all the high school sports in the area, not simply one sport. Much of the way in which assignments are given depends on both the experience of a particular writer and budget and staffing constraints.

Sports columnists are sportswriters who write opinion pieces for publication in newspapers or magazines. Some columnists work for syndicates, which are organizations that sell articles to many media at once. Sports columnists often take stories and enhance the facts with personal opinions and panache. They may also write from their personal experiences. Either way, a column usually has a punchy start, a pithy middle, and a strong, sometimes poignant, ending.

"A well-written column gets right to the point," says Rick Telander, an award-winning sports journalist who currently writes for the *Chicago Sun-Times*, a daily newspaper that serves the Chicagoland area with a circulation of approximately 383,000. (Visit http://www.suntimes.com/index/telander.html to read his columns.) "It doesn't waste words dancing around, though words should be used that make people think or smile or chuckle or wince. There should be a basic point that follows the introduction, backed up not just with opinion, but also with facts (the ones you want to use to make your point). Forget the facts that contradict your point. Others will get those. And then there should be a snappy or thoughtful ending that wraps things up. I always make a tiny outline—maybe just three points. But it helps. My definition of column writing: Say hello. Do a somersault. Say goodbye."

Sports columnists are responsible for writing columns on a regular basis in accordance with a schedule, depending on the frequency of publication. They may write a column daily, weekly, quarterly, or monthly. Like other journalists, they face pressure to meet a deadline.

Most sports columnists are free to select their own story ideas. The need to constantly come up with new and interesting ideas may be one of the hardest parts of the job, but also one of the most rewarding. Columnists search through newspapers, magazines, and the Internet, attend sporting events, watch television, and listen to the radio.

Next, they do research, delving into a topic much like an investigative reporter would, so that they can back up their arguments with facts.

Finally, they write, usually on a computer. After a column is written, at least one editor goes over it to check for clarity and correct mistakes. Then the cycle begins again. Often a sports columnist writes a few relatively timeless pieces to keep for use as backups in a pinch, in case a new idea can't be found or falls through.

Most sports columnists work in newsrooms or magazine offices, although some, especially those who are syndicated but not affiliated with a particular newspaper, work out of their homes or private offices.

Newspapers often run small pictures of sports columnists, called head shots, next to their columns. This, and a consistent placement of a column in a particular spot in the paper, usually gives a sports columnist greater recognition than a reporter or editor.

Like other journalists, sportswriters work in a variety of conditions—the air-conditioned offices of a newsroom or magazine publisher, the sweaty, humid locker room of a professional basketball team, or the arid and dusty field where a baseball team's spring training is held. Sportswriters work irregular hours, putting in as much or as little time as a story requires, often traveling to small towns and out-of-the-way locales to cover a team's away games.

The benefits are obvious—for the individuals who love sports, the job offers the chance to cover sports events every day; to immerse themselves in the statistics and injury lists and bidding wars of professional and amateur sports; to speak, sometimes one on one, with the greatest athletes of yesterday, today, and tomorrow.

WHAT IS IT LIKE TO BE A SPORTSWRITER?

Phil Arvia is a sports columnist for the *Daily Southtown*, a newspaper in Chicago's south suburbs with a circulation of about 50,000. He has been writing about sports since first working as a stringer at a suburban twice-weekly newspaper while in high school in 1979, and has worked full time for newspapers since February 1985. (Visit http://www.dailysouthtown.com/index/dspro.html to read his columns.) "I was lousy in math and science and was impressing teachers in English class ever since elementary school," he recalls, "so writing was in my future. I was also a huge sports fan. After winning a high school writing contest with a journal entry, I got on the school newspaper, and shortly thereafter got a job stringing for a local twice-weekly (*Star Publications*, then based in Chicago Heights). Since *Rolling Stone* never came calling, I stuck with sports."

Phil starts his morning, whether he is writing a column or not, by watching ESPN's SportsCenter and reading two newspapers (the *Daily Southtown* and the *Chicago Tribune*). He then reads the other Chicago-area papers online, and checks his e-mail. Phil's columns appear in Sunday, Monday, Wednesday, and Friday editions of the paper, and he is usu-ally off work on Mondays and Wednesdays. "I try to set up a tentative schedule each week," he says, "which I typically e-mail to my bosses on Monday. My columns, perhaps more than most columnists, tend to be event driven (I like to get to games and talk to people rather than pontificate from my home or office). So, let's say it's a White Sox game day. I arrive at the park by 3:30 (which, for a 7:05 P.M. game, is when the clubhouse opens for interviews). I'll talk to whichever players or coaches I'm interested in talking with that day (or, some days, whoever's available). The manager usually has a press conference during pregame stretching, usually between 4:45 and 5:15. After that, I go upstairs to the press box to transcribe tape. After the home team's batting practice, I pop back downstairs to talk to anyone else I might need. The clubhouse closes an hour before game time, so that's dinnertime. After that, I get back in my spot for game time, and start writing my column, while keeping score and/or going online for research. When the game ends around 10, I go downstairs and get postgame comments, if necessary. I drop those into the column where necessary and file my column before the 10:45 deadline."

DO I HAVE WHAT IT TAKES TO BE A SPORTSWRITER?

Clearly, the ability to write well and concisely is a key requirement for the job of the sportswriter. In addition, you must have a solid understanding of the rules and play of many different sports. If you hope to specialize in the coverage of one particular sport, your knowledge of that sport has to be equal to that of anyone coaching or playing it at the professional level.

Finally, you must be able to elicit information from a variety of sources, as well as to determine when information being leaked is closer to promotional spin than to fact. Most often, a coach or agent does not want to comment for a story on the record, so the sportswriter must be assertive in pressing the source for more information.

Being a columnist requires similar characteristics to those required for being a general sportswriter. But as a columnist, you must also possess a certain wit and

---

To Be a Successful Sportswriter, You Should . . .

- have strong writing skills
- have a love of sports
- have a solid understanding of the rules and play of many different sports
- be assertive and tenacious when interviewing sometimes uncooperative athletes
- have strong communication skills
- be willing to work odd or long hours to cover sporting events
- be able to work under deadline pressure

---

wisdom, the compunction to express strong opinions, and the ability to take apart an issue and debate it.

HOW DO I BECOME A SPORTSWRITER?
Education
High School
English, journalism, and speech are the most important classes for you to take in high school. You will need to master the art of writing in order to be able to convey your ideas concisely, yet creatively, to your readers. Rick Telander encourages high school students to read as much as possible. "Don't just read the sports pages," he advises. "In fact, read novels, great books, intellectual magazines, science books, etc.; that is the general knowledge that will assist your sportswriting. Remember, *everybody* knows the scores and *everybody* has seen the highlights."

Speech classes will also help you become comfortable interacting with others. Be sure to take physical education classes and participate in organized sports, whether as a competitor, a team manager, or an assistant. You also should join the staff of your school paper or yearbook. This will give you a chance to cover and write about your school's sports teams or other school activities.

Postsecondary Training
You will need at least a bachelor's degree to become a sportswriter, although many sportswriters go on to study journalism at the graduate level. Most sportswriters concentrate on journalism while in col-

lege, either by attending a program in journalism or by taking whatever courses are available outside of a specialized program. This isn't to say that you can't become a sportswriter without a degree in journalism, but competition for sportswriting jobs is incredibly fierce. And why wouldn't it be? Sportswriters get great seats at sports events, and they have the credentials to interview sports celebrities. Increasingly, a specialized education is becoming the means by which sports editors and managers sift through the stacks of résumés from prospective sportswriters. Sportswriters may have degrees in communications or English, among other majors.

Internships and Volunteerships

You will likely be required to participate in an internship as part of your college curriculum. This hands-on work experience at a newspaper or magazine will give you the opportunity to work side by side with sportswriters and other professionals. Internships routinely last 4 to 12 months and count toward semester credit hours.

You can learn on-the-job skills by working for your high school and college newspapers. The experience can be related to sports, of course, but any journalistic experience will help you develop the basic skills useful to any reporter, regardless of the area about which you are writing.

You can increase your chances and success in the field by applying to colleges or universities with renowned academic programs in journalism. Most accredited

programs have a required period of training in which you will intern with a major newspaper somewhere in the United States; student interns are responsible for covering a beat.

You may also find it helpful to read publications that are related to this field, such as *Sports Illustrated* (http://sportsillustrated.cnn.com) and *Sports Business*

The Pros and Cons of Being a Sports Columnist

The editors of *What Can I Do Now?: Sports* asked Phil Arvia, a sports columnist for the *Daily Southtown*, to describe the pros and cons of being a sportswriter.

Pros:

- It's not manual labor.

- You get to do a lot of travel.

- You meet tons of very interesting people.

- A lot of people value your opinion.

- You get to witness the greatest athletes in the world doing truly breathtaking things.

Cons:

- A lot of people think you're an idiot, and don't hesitate to tell you.

- You're always working nights and weekends.

- There's a lot of travel.

- The athletes are irritated by your presence.

- The pay isn't great.

Journal (http://www.sportsbusinessjournal.com), and to visit Web sites such as the Associated Press Sports Editors (http://apse.dallasnews.com).

WHO WILL HIRE ME?

Sportswriters are employed by newspapers and magazines throughout the world. They may cover professional teams based in large cities or high school teams located in tiny towns. Sportswriters also work as freelance writers.

You may have to begin your career as a sportswriter by covering the games or matches that no else wants to or can cover. As a stringer, you won't earn much money and you'll probably have a second or even third job, but eventually it may lead to covering bigger and better games and teams. Some sportswriters make a living covering sports for very small towns; others only work at those jobs until they have gained the experience to move on.

Most journalists start their careers by working in small markets—little towns and cities with local papers. You may work for a newspaper for a year or two and then apply for positions with larger papers in bigger towns and cities. Sportswriters for newspapers follow the same routine, and more than a few end up pursuing areas other than sports because the job openings in sports simply weren't there. The lucky few who hang on to a small sports beat can often parlay that beat into a better position by sticking with the job and demonstrating a devotion to the sport, even cultivating a following of loyal fans. This could lead to a full-time column.

Most likely, as a sportswriter, you will take advantage of opportunities to learn more about athletes and sports in general. Becoming an expert on a little-known but rapidly growing sport may be one way for you to do this. For example, if you were to learn all that you can about mountain biking, you might be able to land a job with one of the magazines specializing in the sport of mountain biking.

Competition for full-time jobs with magazines as a sportswriter is just as keen as it is for major newspapers. Often, a sportswriter will write articles and try to sell them to one of the major magazines, hoping that when an opening comes, he or she will have first crack at it. Still, most sportswriters move into the world of sports magazines after they've proven themselves in newspaper sportswriting. It is possible, however, to get a job with a sports magazine straight from college or graduate school; it is more likely that you'll have to work your way up.

The career services offices of colleges or universities with accredited undergraduate and graduate programs in journalism can be extremely helpful in beginning your job search. In fact, many graduates of these programs are not only highly sought after by newspapers and magazines, but these graduates are also often offered jobs by the newspapers and magazines for which they interned during school.

WHERE CAN I GO FROM HERE?

The constraints of budget, staffing, and time—which make a sportswriter's job difficult—are also often what can help a sportswriter rise through the ranks. For example, the writer asked to cover all the sports in a small area may have to hustle to cover the beat alone, but that writer also won't have any competition when covering the big events. Thus, he or she can gain valuable experience and bylines writing for a small paper, whereas in a larger market, the same sportswriter would have to wait much longer to be assigned an event that might result in a coveted byline.

Sportswriters advance by gaining the top assignments, covering the major sports in feature articles, as opposed to the bare-bones summaries of events. They also advance by moving to larger and larger papers, by getting columns, and finally, by getting a syndicated column—that is, a column carried by many papers around the country or even around the world.

Sportswriters for magazines advance by moving up the publishing ladder, from editorial assistant to associate editor to writer. Often, an editorial assistant might be assigned to research a story for a sports brief—a quirky or short look at an element of the game. For example, *Sports Illustrated* might have a page devoted to new advances in sports equipment for the amateur athlete. The editorial assistant might be given the idea and asked to research the topic. A writer might eventually write it up, using the editorial assistant's notes. Advancement, then, comes in being actually listed as the author of the piece.

In the publishing worlds of both newspapers and magazines, sportswriters can advance by becoming editors of a newspaper's sports page or of a sports magazine. There are also *sports publicists* and *sports information directors* who work for the publicity and promotions arms of colleges, universities, and professional sports teams. These individuals release statements, write and disseminate to the press articles on the organizations' teams and athletes, and arrange press opportunities for coaches and athletes.

"In 10 years," says Rick Telander, "I'll be 67 and retired! But I can't imagine that I'll ever stop writing for somebody—even if just to myself. My retirement will be full of good times and adventure."

In 5 or 10 years, Phil Arvia says that he will probably be "blogging or providing content for some 24-hour, online mutation of what I do now, and not being very happy about it. Or, blogging or providing content for some 24-hour, online mutation of the parent paper in

Related Jobs

- columnists
- essayists
- foreign correspondents
- magazine editors
- newspaper editors
- online journalists
- reporters
- sports information directors
- sports publicists

the *Southtown*'s news group (the *Chicago Sun-Times*) and being quite content."

WHAT ARE THE SALARY RANGES?

According the U.S. Department of Labor, writers earned median annual earnings of $45,460 in 2004. The lowest 10 percent earned less than $23,700, while the highest 10 percent earned $87,660 or more. The median annual salary for all writers in the newspaper and book publishing industries was $45,450.

Sportswriters who cover the major sports events, who have their own column, or who have a syndicated column can expect to earn more. Sportswriters who write for major magazines can also expect to earn more, sometimes on a per-article basis, depending on their reputations and the contracts that they or their agents have negotiated.

WHAT IS THE JOB OUTLOOK?

The turnover rate for top sportswriters with major newspapers and magazines isn't very high, which means that job openings occur as sportswriters retire, die, are fired, or move into other markets. While the publishing industry may have room for yet another magazine devoted to a particular sports specialty, competition for sportswriting jobs will continue to be strong through 2014 and beyond.

Umpires and Referees

SUMMARY

Definition
Umpires and referees enforce the rules of a sport during the event. Their decisions are binding and they have the power to penalize athletes, coaches, and teams.

Alternative Job Titles
Judges

Linesmen
Sports officials

Salary Range
$14,000 to $21,000 to $300,000+

Educational Requirements
High school diploma

Certification or Licensing
Required

Employment Outlook
Faster than the average

High School Subjects
Foreign language
Physical education
Speech

Personal Interests
Exercise/personal fitness
Sports
Travel

"It takes a lot of courage for referees to get out in the middle of a competition between two teams that both desperately want to win and have your judgment be publicly scrutinized week in and week out," says Sandra Hunt, a referee for the U.S. Soccer Federation. "I admire referees in all sports, at all levels, who conduct themselves with such grace under fire."

WHAT DO UMPIRES AND REFEREES DO?

Umpires and referees work on the playing field or court during a sporting event to enforce the rules. They observe the players and events of the game and make split-second decisions about plays and disputable circumstances. They may penalize teams or players for breaking rules or behaving in an improper manner, and may even eject players or coaches from the game. Umpires and referees are responsible for ending arguments on the court or field and may stop play in a game. They use a standard set of hand signals to explain their rulings and decisions to viewers.

Umpires and referees, who both fall under the job title "sports official," work in nearly all sports and at all levels of sports. Usually they officiate in pairs or groups, but many youth and amateur events only have one referee or umpire per game. Umpires and referees work for a sports organization such as the National

Hockey League, the Pac-10 College Conference, or a state's interscholastic athletic commission. They do not follow a specific sports team from game to game but rather each crew of officials has its own schedule. In this way, the officials' crew is akin to the players' team.

Major-league baseball umpires work and travel in a crew of four, one for each base and home plate. Rookie through triple-A professional baseball leagues employ three umpires per game, leaving second base without an official. These umpires rotate through the bases clockwise after each game. Home plate umpires determine whether pitched balls are thrown through the strike zone, keep a count of balls and strikes, and determine whether runners crossing home plate are safe or out. Umpires at the bases also determine whether runners are safe or out on base, and first and third base umpires must decide whether a batted ball is in fair territory. During the World Series, two more umpires work along the foul lines in the outfield.

Seven officials work on the field during games of the National Football League. Unlike baseball officials who are all called umpires and who work all of the bases on rotation, football officials have different titles depending on the area in which they work. The *referee* works behind the offensive team watching for illegal moves, and it is his or her role to signal fouls and penalties to the coaches and scorers. Although all football officials may call penalties, the referee is ultimately in charge and has the final say.

The umpire in football stands on the defensive side and looks for illegal blocks or other fouls. The *head lines official* marks the progress of the ball and supervises the chain crew, who records downs and marks the yardage gained or lost. The *line judge* times the game, the *field judge* makes calls on pass interference, and the *back and side judges* make calls on receivers and sideline plays. Football officials blow whistles to stop play in order to measure the progress of the ball, to communicate penalties, or to announce that a player has been injured.

National Basketball Association games are worked by three officials, a lead official and two others. These officials run up and down the court with the players, keeping an eye on the ball and looking out for illegal actions by the players. One official stays near the basket of the offense, another stands even with the free throw line, and the third is stationed opposite the second official nearer mid-court. Because of where they are positioned, each official watches for different things. For example, the official near the offensive team's basket ensures that no offensive player stands in the free throw lane for more than three seconds.

Professional hockey games have three officials who skate along with the players. The referee, who is the lead official, calls penalties. The two linesmen call offsides and icing and govern face-offs.

Four people officiate at professional soccer games; the referee and two linesmen work on the field making calls, and another official works the sidelines and is in charge of substitutions and monitoring the benches. Off the field, court, or rink, umpires and referees prepare balls for play, discuss rule interpretations, and attend clinics and seminars to keep up to date.

Sports officials work wherever the sport is being played. For hockey and basketball officials, this is indoors at the court or rink. Professional football and baseball, traditionally outdoor sports, are now played both indoors and outdoors, depending on the venue. For example, baseball's Minnesota Twins play indoors at the Metrodome and the Atlanta Falcons host National Football League games indoors at the Georgia Dome. On the college, high school, youth, and amateur levels, football and baseball continue to be outdoor sports. Some hockey at these levels is also played outdoors.

Officials who work in sports that are played outdoors must contend with heat, rain, and snow, all while wearing uniforms that may not be suitable for the conditions. Whereas baseball games may be rained out, a football game is almost never canceled due to weather.

Sports officials work a combination of afternoons, nights, and weekends. In addition, many sports are played on holidays when fans can attend. Depending on the sport and the level, umpires and referees may work only one game a week or as many as six. Umpires and referees in college, amateur, and youth sports are hired on a per-game basis and typically have other jobs.

Because they are out on the court, field, rink, or ring with the athletes, sports officials do run the risk of injury. They might be hit by a ball, bumped by a player, or

---

Lingo to Learn

boundaries The limits or edges of a playing field or court.

call A decision or ruling made by an official.

foul An infraction of the rules.

foul ball In baseball, a ball hit outside of the first or third base line; not in fair territory.

line of scrimmage In football, an imaginary line where the ball is placed before each down and where the offense and defense meet.

offsides A rule violation in which an offensive player crosses the line of scrimmage ahead of the ball or puck.

penalty A disadvantage, such as a loss of yardage, time, points, or possession of the ball imposed on a team or competitor for violating a rule.

---

injured while running. Unfortunately, too, when umpires and referees make calls that displease athletes, coaches, or fans, they run the risk of being victims of unsportsmanlike behavior such as assault or harassment.

WHAT IS IT LIKE TO BE AN UMPIRE OR REFEREE?

Sandra Hunt has been a U.S. Soccer Federation (USSF) referee since 1987. She currently works as an instructor for referee development and referee assessment on contracted status for the USSF Referee Department and also the Federation

International Football Association (FIFA), which is headquartered in Zurich, Switzerland. "I did not know at the time I began refereeing," she says, "that this would lead to a job both domestically and internationally. While I was still an active FIFA international referee, I was asked to begin instructing at referee clinics and tournaments in the United States. These assignments lead to exposure as an instructor and assessor at the international level. I am really enjoying the challenge of instructing and 'coaching' referees both in the United States and internationally. It is a great honor and privilege to be associated with so many fine people."

Sandra receives an instructional assignment at least six weeks in advance of the training session. "I make early contact with the local administrators to confirm the content of what I will present to make sure it is interesting and relevant for their participants. Up until the time I travel to the venue, I spend a good bit of time organizing my material. My main duty, I feel, is to offer clear instruction and interpretation to referees, in order to make their on-field duties and responsibilities easier to perform. Secondly, I feel it is my responsibility to let them know how important they are to U.S. Soccer and to support their participation and dedication to the game and the players they serve."

Sandra works both indoors and outdoors. Both U.S. Soccer and FIFA offer instructional sessions, which are presented in the classroom and on the field of play. "Classroom sessions," she explains, "often consist of PowerPoint presentations, which include video clips of game situations that are discussed in order to find solutions. Referees, assessors, and instructors who are participating in the course are encouraged to ask questions to achieve clarification on all materials. The outdoor sessions involve active participation on a field of play where current procedures, mechanics, and instruction in a more dynamic setting can take place. This is an opportunity to see referees in action and to observe their abilities in a simulated game setting."

Sandra travels often for her job. "I am away from home many weekends and at least four full weeks each year, sometimes more."

Marcy Weston has been involved in organized athletics since she was in junior high school. She served as the national coordinator of women's basketball, officiating for the National Collegiate Athletic Association for 21 years, before retiring at the end of 2005. She also coached field hockey, volleyball, and basketball at the college level. Marcy is currently the senior associate director of athletics at Central Michigan University in Mt. Pleasant, Michigan. "I've spent over 40 years of my life as an official and coordinator," she says, "and have loved virtually every minute of my work in both of those roles. The skills I've developed have enhanced my work as a coach and as an administrator. I've learned how to negotiate, listen, be flexible, and how to cope with stress and adversarial situations. I can tell you for a fact that making calls in two NCAA national championship games prepares you for just about any stressful sports-

To Be a Successful Umpire or Referee, You Should . . .

- be mature and independent in your thinking
- be self-confident and absolutely firm when making a call
- be in good physical condition
- have good communication skills and be able to get along with players, managers, and colleagues alike
- enjoy traveling

related situation. Officiating allows you to stay in shape, earn some great money, and play a role in the game that is essential—managing a sport contest. It takes skill, savvy, and a passion for the sport."

DO I HAVE WHAT IT TAKES TO BE AN UMPIRE OR REFEREE?

Umpires and referees are mature and independent. They should be able to follow their schedules and get themselves to games without supervision. Umpires and referees must also be independent in their thinking, employing an unwavering self-confidence that makes their decisions the final word.

Umpires and referees cannot be timid. They must have strong personalities in order to keep total control of the game. At moments where a call is unpopular

and fans are booing, players complaining, and coaches shouting, umpires and referees must be able to remain calm and stand by their judgment. This trait is important at any level of sports, as even an angry Little Leaguer can be quite vocal. Sports officials need to maintain their strength and confidence, though, without becoming arrogant.

Officials in all sports should be good communicators who can make their judgments clear and grammatically correct. Because many professional baseball players speak Spanish and many hockey players are French or Russian speakers, officials in these sports should be able to communicate in these languages as well.

Sports officials should be in good physical shape with excellent endurance, and those who work in hockey must be outstanding skaters. Because umpires and referees cannot let their minds wander during a game, people who work in this career need excellent powers of concentration.

Umpires and referees need the ability to get along well with other people. At all levels of sports they work closely with coaches and players from a wide variety of backgrounds and cultures.

"A sports official," says Marcy Weston, "needs to be honest, have integrity, demonstrate a sense of fairness, possess negotiating skills, have a sense of humor, and love the game. These qualities are necessary to manage the pace, pressure, and rigors in the life of a sports official."

Sandra Hunt believes that individuals with many of the following traits make strong referees: honesty, integrity, humility, kindness, unshakable values,

Advice to Aspiring Sports Officials

● ● ● ● ● ● ● ●

Sandra Hunt offers the following advice to high school students who are interested in becoming soccer referees:

- Play the game of soccer at the highest level you can. Playing experience will be extremely useful if you intend to referee at the professional level.

- Get started as an entry-level referee. Find a mentor—someone with experience who will commit to working with you and providing constructive feedback on a somewhat regular basis. As referees move up through the levels of refereeing, they need additional mentors with experience at the higher levels of the game.

- Be ready to laugh at yourself early and often. You will make mistakes—many in public, unfortunately. The referees who advance to the top are the ones who recognize that fact and persevere.

- Be humble and be kind. No referee has ever had a perfect game.

firm character, strong constitution, self-discipline, commitment, compassion, confidence, respect, insight, cleverness, and a good sense of humor.

HOW DO I BECOME AN UMPIRE OR A REFEREE?

Education

High School

If you are interested in becoming an umpire or referee you should begin learning as much as you can about sports and their rules. You will also want to get in the physical shape necessary to keep up with the athletes during an event. The most obvious way to accomplish these goals is to participate in school sports.

In class, you will want to focus on English grammar and also other languages if you are interested in working as a baseball umpire or hockey official. Speech, debate, or theater courses will build your self-confidence and teach you the diction skills you need to be understood clearly.

Finally, sports bring together many kinds of people, and as an umpire or referee you must be diplomatic with all of them. Classes in sociology, history, and psychology can help you learn about the different cultures and ways of thinking of people from all parts of the world.

Postsecondary Training

Although umpires and referees are not required to attend four-year colleges or universities, many do have college degrees. Often sports officials are former college athletes who decided to pursue a career in sports in a nonperformance capacity. Obviously, attending college and participating in college athletics is an excellent way to reinforce your knowledge of a sport and its rules while receiving a solid education.

In almost all cases, officials must attend special training schools or complete courses. These can vary from the schools endorsed by the Major League's Umpire Development Program all the way to the training courses offered to officials in amateur softball. These schools and training courses can be contacted through professional and amateur leagues, college athletic conferences, and state interscholastic commissions. These organizations can also inform you of minimum age requirements (usually 18 and out of high school) and other criteria that vary between leagues and sports.

Certification or Licensing

The special training programs that umpires and referees attend act as their certification. Without these, they are not eligible to officiate. These courses may vary from those in the official training schools of professional umpires to those courses taken through a state interscholastic athletic commission for middle school volleyball officials.

Internships and Volunteerships

High school students interested in becoming officials should experiment with umpiring or refereeing youth sports. Even if you work as a volunteer you will be gaining valuable knowledge of an official's job. Contact local youth leagues such as Little League or American Youth Soccer Association for information on officiating in your area. Summer camps and after-school recreation programs also offer excellent opportunities for you to try organizing and officiating youth sports. Community centers such as the YMCA or the Jewish Community Center, churches, and local elementary schools can be excellent sources of information for finding these opportunities.

Labor Unions

Some sports officials are unionized while others are not. In professional baseball, for example, the World Umpires Association represents major-league umpires, while the Association of Minor League Umpires represents minor-league umpires. Officials in amateur sports are typically not unionized.

WHO WILL HIRE ME?

Marcy Weston was introduced to the field via an officiating class she took during her sophomore year in college. "My instructor thought two of us were pretty good and invited us to work a game with her," she recalls. "The other student and I officiated the junior varsity game, and each of us worked one half of the varsity game with the instructor. From there on, I worked some high school and college games along with a hospital nurses league in Ohio, which was equivalent to working small college games. I was assigned college games three or four years later, and then my career started to move forward rather quickly."

Because they must be unbiased, umpires and referees are hired by sports leagues, associations, and commissions rather than by specific teams. These governing bodies screen and train potential officials and then hire them to work in the sport. Olympic officials, too, are appointed from the league or governing body of the sport for which they work.

Umpires and referees do not step into professional training programs without some background experience, and this experience is gained by officiating amateur, high school, and then college events. For example, officials for the National

Football League must have at least 10 years of experience before applying to the league, and at least 5 of those years must be in prominent college competition.

The first step toward becoming an umpire or referee is to contact your state interscholastic athletic commission. The commission can inform you of the requirements for becoming a middle or high school official in your state and enroll you in courses and exams specific to your sport. After completing the requisite steps, the commission will certify you as an official in your sport and begin hiring you to officiate on a per-game basis. During this time you will be gaining the experience you need to move toward college or professional sports, if this is your goal.

Those interested in officiating in amateur sports such as adult baseball, softball, and soccer leagues should contact city leagues, recreation centers, and sports parks in their area.

WHERE CAN I GO FROM HERE?

The natural progression for umpires and referees is to begin by officiating young peoples' games and advance to amateur adults' contests. Those with talent and determination may move on to college games or professional minor leagues.

Many officials who would like to move to the professional level attend umpire or referee camps. Many of these camps are conducted by professional officials. These programs feature a rigorous review of rules and regulations and often include game situations.

The minor leagues in baseball are a testing ground for prospective umpires. On average, umpires spend six to eight years at the minor-league level before they are even considered for a major-league position. Hockey and soccer also have minor leagues throughout the United States, and officials in these sports work their way through a system similar to that of professional baseball. Football and basketball officials advance through the ranks of high school, amateur, and college sports, spending at least five years at the college level before moving on.

Once officials have succeeded in reaching professional sports, they might begin advancing within that realm. Sports officials who become particularly successful may be invited to work tournaments or special events such as the All-Star game, Super Bowl, World Cup, or even the

Advancement Possibilities

lead or *head officials supervise the other* members of an officiating team.

umpire or *referee training school instructors* or *directors* teach others the officiating skills necessary to be successful officials.

head officials for college athletic associations are responsible for the training, scheduling, and supervision of sports officials at the collegiate level.

Olympics. They may also advance (like Sandra Hunt) to teaching in or directing a training program for other officials, or, like Marcy Weston, they may go on to supervise sports officials for a collegiate or professional sports association.

Many umpires and referees who work at the amateur and youth levels choose not to advance but stay at those levels simply because they love it. These workers usually have other jobs that may be entirely unrelated to the sports industry, and do their officiating on evenings and weekends as a kind of paid hobby.

In the next 5 or 10 years, Sandra Hunt hopes to remain healthy and able to continue instructing soccer referees. "I would like to continue to work for both the USSF Referee Department and the FIFA for as long as they believe I am able to make a contribution. With their blessing, I am 'a lifer.'"

Marcy Weston plans to continue working as the senior associate director of athletics at Central Michigan University until she retires in the next four or five years.

WHAT ARE THE SALARY RANGES?

Umpire and referee salaries vary greatly, depending on the sport and the level at which it is played. Typically, the closer an official gets to the top of a professional sports league, the higher the wages, but this is not always the case. For example, some college basketball referees might earn more money than a nonlead official in a less popular professional sport.

The U.S. Department of Labor reports median annual earnings of $21,730 for umpires and related workers in 2004. Salaries ranged from less than $14,540 to more than $44,330.

According to the Professional Baseball Umpire Corporation, umpire salaries ranged from $1,800 to $2,000 per month in the Rookie League to $2,500 to $3,400 per month in the triple-A league to a starting annual salary of $84,000 (in 2003) for a major-league umpire. Major-league umpires with considerable experience can earn more than $300,000 a year. Professional basketball officials' salaries range from $77,000 to about $224,000, depending on the experience of the official.

Officials in the National Football League are considered part-time employees who are paid by the game and do not receive benefits. The league cites 2000 salaries as ranging from $1,500 to $4,000 per game, depending on experience.

In professional sports, umpires and referees are typically given additional money for travel, hotel, and food expenses. These officials also receive extra payment if they are invited to work special events such as the World Series or Stanley Cup Finals. Football officials who work the Super Bowl, for example, are paid approximately $12,000.

Umpires and referees at the college, amateur, and youth levels are paid by the game. College officials earn between $200 and $800 per game, and high school and middle school officials earn considerably less. A state interscholastic athletic commission might pay officials $19 to $25 per game, depending on the sport.

Related Jobs

- clockers
- coaches
- flaggers
- lead pony riders
- league or association commissioners
- pit stewards
- professional athletes
- race starters
- race timers
- sports judges
- sports statisticians
- team general managers

WHAT IS THE JOB OUTLOOK?

The growth outlook for the field of sports officiating depends on the sport and the league worked. Umpires and referees are almost always needed at the youth, high school, and amateur levels, and people who are interested in supplementing their incomes this way or simply learning about the field of officiating should find plenty of opportunities for work, especially part-time work.

In professional sports the market is much tighter. Umpires in the major leagues rarely leave the job except to retire. In fact, during a 10-year period, the American League hired only three new umpires. When an opening does occur, an umpire moves up from triple-A baseball, creating an opening for an umpire from double-A, and so on. Professional sports without minor leagues offer even fewer employment opportunities for officials at the professional level. The creation of new expansion teams (such as baseball's Arizona Diamondbacks and hockey's Columbus Blue Jackets) and new leagues (such as the Women's National Basketball Association and the National Pro Fastpitch League [softball]) does occasionally offer additional job opportunities for professional sports officials.

The outlook for female sports officials has improved in recent years with the creation of women's professional basketball leagues such as the WNBA, offering many new positions to women officials, as well as coaches, trainers, and professional athletes. Additionally, in 1997, two women, Dee Kantner and Violet Palmer, became the first female referees to officiate NBA basketball games—a first for the all-male U.S. major sports leagues. Perhaps more openings for women officials will be created in the future as the other leagues follow suit.

SECTION 3

Do It Yourself

Careers in professional sports don't happen overnight. On the contrary, they result from years of practice, hard work, commitment, and experience. These same careers don't happen only to the athletes who wear the uniforms; they happen to thousands of individuals who, like you, love sports and the challenge of competition, but who contribute to the world of professional sports in ways which utilize their unique talents and abilities. In fact, many professional athletes turn to some of these sports-related careers once their playing days are over.

The single best thing you can do now is to find a sport that you love—to play or watch—and get involved with it at some level, whether it's coaching a soccer team of eight-year-olds or playing a varsity sport in high school. Most high schools support a variety of popular sports, including football, basketball, baseball, softball, soccer, field hockey, track and field, volleyball, golf, wrestling, swimming, gymnastics, tennis, cross country, and ice hockey. Many of these are also supported through the lower grade levels. Other sports, such as rowing, lacrosse, horseback riding, and badminton, for example, might not be as popular in your area of the country, but don't let a lack of popularity stop you from participating in a sport.

While it's true that the most popular high school sports—football, baseball, basketball, and hockey—are also the most popular professional sports, you shouldn't give up on something you truly enjoy merely because of your future prospects of finding a job. Your knowledge and first-hand experience with a sport will go a long way toward helping you forge a career in that sport. And you never know how the job market will change. Many sports experience a sudden groundswell in support as a result of increased media coverage or an Olympic victory. Gymnastics and figure skating, for example, are two sports that have benefited greatly from Americans winning Olympic gold medals. All of which goes to show that if you want to pursue a career related to a sport, don't go with the odds: follow your heart.

❏ PLAY A SPORT

Even if your ultimate goal is not playing a sport at a professional level, it never hurts to develop an understanding of the game, its rules, and the people who play it. So go ahead and have some fun. Participate in a team or individual sport that you enjoy. Who knows? You might just have what it takes to compete one day at a professional level. And if not, you've only gained good health and a wealth of wonderful friends and memories, as well as insight that may help you develop a career related to sports.

❏ JOIN AN EXISTING TEAM

Regardless of your grade level in school, there are ample opportunities to learn to play a sport. Most grade schools, junior high schools, and high schools sponsor a variety of team sports, from football, basketball, and swimming to soccer, wrestling, track, and gymnastics. If a team sport does not exist in your school, that doesn't mean your chances at playing it have evaporated. Petition your school board to establish it as a school sport and set aside funds for it. In the meantime, organize other students into a club team, scheduling practices and unofficial games. If the sport is a recognized team sport in the United States and Canada, contact the professional organization for the sport for additional information; if anyone has helpful tips for gaining recognition, the professional organization does. Also, try calling the local or state athletic board to see what other schools in your area recognize it as a team sport; make a list of those teams and try scheduling exhibition games with them. Your goal is to show that other students have a definite interest in the game, and that other schools recognize it.

Teams in many of these sports are also sponsored by community organizations, such as YMCAs and YWCAs, churches, youth groups, and parks and recreation services, as well as by private companies.

Experiment with a variety of sports. Now is the best time to try out for different sports and discover what you like and what you're good at. Many students participate in a different sport each season; tennis in the fall, basketball during the winter, and baseball or softball in the spring. Even if you end up concentrating later in life on only one of the sports, as is usual, playing a variety of sports will enhance your coordination, improve your health, and augment your knowledge of sports in general.

Finally, stick with whatever sport you enjoy and learn the complexities of it.

Many students who lacked coordination and timing in grade school and junior high school find that, by the time they reach high school, they have developed in these areas and can participate in sports. Don't believe that simply because you were cut from one team means you have no talent or can't try out again. Too many kids give up and spend the rest of their high school years looking on longingly as others go on to play.

❑ START YOUR OWN TEAM

Other sports, such as figure skating, for example, may require that you seek out the services of a specialized coach or trainer in the sport in order to take lessons and practice. However, wherever there are ice rinks there are also others, like you, who like to skate, and many teams of skaters also exist. Check with the rinks in your area for more information.

It's relatively easy to find teams for the most popular sports, like football or basketball. What do you do when you're interested in lacrosse or rowing, or even badminton, let alone mountain biking or extreme skiing? To find existing teams playing these sports is more difficult, and often, impossible. Don't let that stop you. Post signs in your school or take out an ad in the school paper, and try to discover if there's anyone else out there who is also interested in the sport. If this doesn't work, broaden the area of your search with signs or ads in the local gym, YMCA, or town newspaper. Chances are, you'll find at least one person who also shares the same interest in the sport.

If you're lucky, you'll discover that there are a lot of kids who would be interested in the sport. Once you know there's an interest, find a reliable teacher or adult who is experienced in the sport, or who is willing to learn more. With even a small group, you can schedule practices and competitions. If you're still stuck and need further ideas or contacts, get in touch with the national or professional association of the sport and see if they can help you out. Organizations like these are usually eager to help foster and promote interest in their sport, so they may send someone to talk to your group, or even donate equipment or refer you to a coach.

Participating in one or more sports is not only good for your physical and mental health, but it's also a way of socializing with others and sharing the love of a particular endeavor. Perhaps the single best thing you can derive from learning and participating in a sport is how to pursue an activity that will give you great pleasure for the rest of your life. If you are exceptionally gifted at the sport you love, then you might seriously consider a career as a professional athlete.

❑ VOLUNTEER WITH A TEAM

If you can't participate in a sport, but you still want to stay involved, there are many opportunities for you, too. For example, many school teams and club sports need help with everyday management such as organizing the athletic equipment used in practices or competitions, assisting with drills and other routines during practices, taping and wrapping ankles, and making sure each and every team member is back on the bus after an away game.

If your skills and interests are closer to coaching, why not talk to the coach and see if she or he will let you volunteer as an assistant or student coach? Tell the coach you'll help run drills and pass out playbooks. If you're good at these tasks, you might think about a career as a coach. Keep in mind, however, that most coaches have gained a lot of their experience from actually playing the sport.

If you're better with Band-Aids and heating pads, ask the team physician or trainer if you can volunteer as an assistant trainer. You'll gain valuable knowledge as you learn from a professional, as well as the priceless benefits of on-the-job experience. Take CPR classes, spend your summer as a lifeguard, and write to professional trainer organizations for information on how you can gain points toward becoming a trainer through these experiences. If you excel in this area, you may be on your way to becoming a sports physician or athletic trainer.

❑ EXERCISE YOUR VOICE, TOO

Do you love to watch sports and critique the plays and abilities of teams and players? Maybe you should investigate possibilities that lead to a career as a sports broadcaster. Get a head start on the competition and indulge your need to provide your friends with a running commentary by hosting a sports hour on the school radio station. If your school doesn't have a radio station, that's your cue to start one. Nothing looks better on a college or job application than the fact that you had the ambition and initiative, not to mention the organizational abilities, to found a group or activity. While you may be fortunate enough to actually get a frequency assigned (it's not impossible, just requires more work), most high schools use their public address systems to pipe in the "broadcasts" to the student lounge.

Other possibilities include starting your own cable access show and volunteering at a radio or cable television station in the area. Or you could work in print journalism first, by covering high school sports events for the local paper.

❏ THREE STRIKES AND YOU'RE—IN?

Teams can't always afford to pay the officials who referee games and other competitions. If calling the shots—out or in, that is—is more your style, then you might want to begin gaining experience as an umpire or referee.

Local softball leagues, to name but one of many possibilities, are often in need of officials. Check with the athletic clubs in your area to see if they can use a volunteer referee. Who knows? You might even get paid.

Another option is to volunteer with the parks and recreation organization in your area as a summer counselor at one of the parks. Organize games and activities for the kids who participate and judge their progress. Or, think really big and organize a fun meet, complete with relay races and individual medals.

❏ PROFESSIONAL SPORTS LEAGUES, ASSOCIATIONS, AND ORGANIZATIONS

If you are ambitious and want to try something different instead of or in addition to the above possibilities, contact the professional organization for the sport you most enjoy and see if it offers a summer internship or other position. Many are most concerned with employing college students during the summer, but there may be other jobs for which you might qualify, such as bat girl or boy, equipment manager, or public relations gofer. Apply early for the application materials and submit the finished application well in advance of the deadline. Competition for these positions, when available, is incredibly keen.

❏ CONCLUSION

We hope these suggestions have been of some help to you in deciding what activities to consider getting involved with and how best to pursue them. Participating in organized sports means you are learning skills that will not only help you lead a healthy and active life, but also allow you to develop the knowledge and skills that are necessary to pursuing a career in sports, as an athlete or in one of the many careers related to professional sports.

SECTION 4

What Can I Do Right Now?

Get Involved: A Directory of Camps, Programs, And Competitions

As with most other fields, you can prepare for a career in sports right now, while you're still in high school. If you're interested in playing a sport professionally, playing it at the high school level is, of course, one of the best means of preparation. But if you're really serious about your sport and want to do more, or if your sport is not available at school, there are other ways to refine your skills and improve your career prospects. If you don't plan to play a sport professionally but would like to work in a sport in a different capacity, there are also ways to prepare for that.

In the following pages you will find a listing of opportunities designed to help high school students prepare for a career in sports. Some are internships with professional associations, others are camps and clinics for improving athletic abilities, and still others are memberships in organizations that support sporting activities. It's up to you to decide whether you are interested in one particular type of program or are open to a number of possibilities. The types of opportunities available are listed right after the name of the program or organization, so you can skim to find the listings that interest you most.

❑ THE CATEGORIES
Camp/Clinic
When you see an activity that is classified as a camp, don't automatically start packing your tent and mosquito repellent. The term "camp" sometimes simply means a residential program including both educational and recreational activities. A clinic is generally a nonresidential program that concentrates solely on athletic instruction. However, this distinction is not always made and the sponsoring organizations sometimes use the terms interchangeably. Be sure to read the program description carefully so you know exactly what the program entails. For more camps and clinics, visit the following Web sites: http://www.campsearch.com and http://www.petersons.com/high-school/landing.asp?id=872&path=hs.fas.summer&sponsor=1.

College Courses/Summer Study
These terms are linked because most college courses offered to students your age must take place in the summer, when you are out of school. Many colleges and universities sponsor summer study programs in order to attract future students and to give them a head start in higher education. Summer study of almost any

type is a good idea because it keeps your mind and your study skills sharp over the long vacation. Summer study at a college offers any number of additional benefits, including giving you the tools to make a well-informed decision about your future academic career. For more academic programs, visit http://www.petersons.com/highschool/landing.asp?id=872&path=hs.fas.summer.

Competition

Competitions are, of course, the primary way to participate in a sport. Therefore, if you're active in playing a sport, competitions are bound to come your way even if you don't seek them out specially. That's why we're including only a few competitions in this section. But if you do want to compete at a more advanced level than is possible in your area, speak to your instructor about it or contact one of your sport's professional organizations.

Conference

Conferences for high school students are usually difficult to track down because most are for professionals in the field who gather to share new information and ideas with each other. Don't be discouraged, though. A number of professional organizations with student branches invite those student members to their conferences and plan special events for them. Some student branches even run their own conferences; check the directory of student organizations at the end of this section for possible leads. This is an option worth pursuing because conferences focus on some of the most current information available and also give you the chance to meet professionals who can answer your questions and even offer advice.

Employment and Internship Opportunities

As you may already know from experience, employment opportunities for teenagers can be very limited. This is particularly true in a career field as popular as sports. There are a few jobs in the field for high school students, but playing professionally is usually not among them. Every team or stadium does need people to take tickets and sell concessions and souvenirs, so if you want a job in a sporting environment, contact your local team(s) about applying for these jobs.

Basically, an internship combines the responsibilities of a job (strict schedules, pressing duties, and usually written evaluations by your supervisor) with the uncertainties of a volunteer position (no wages or fringe benefits, no guarantee of future employment). That may not sound very enticing, but completing an internship is a great way to prove your maturity, your commitment to your chosen sport, and your knowledge and skills to colleges, potential employers, and yourself.

Unfortunately, internships with professional teams and related organizations are often limited to college students. However, some groups are willing to work with high school students, so it's up to you to convince them that you can be of as much help as an older intern. And even if there is no formal internship available, you can volunteer to help out with mass mailings, errands, or whatever else needs to be done. Be persistent, though professional and polite, and see what happens.

Field Experience

This is something of a catchall category for activities that don't exactly fit the other descriptions. But anything called a field experience in this book is a good opportunity to get involved with the sports industry on some level.

Membership

When an organization appears in this category, it simply means that you are welcome to pay your dues and become a card-carrying member. Formally joining any organization has the benefits of meeting others who share your interests and concerns, finding opportunities to be active, and keeping up with current events in the field and in the group. Depending on how active you are, the contacts you make and experiences you gain may help when the time comes to apply to colleges or look for a job.

In some organizations, you may pay a special student rate but receive virtually the same benefits as a regular adult member. Other groups have student branches with special activities and publications. Don't let membership dues discourage you from contacting any of these organizations. Most charge a low fee because they know that students are perpetually short of funds. If even that is too much for you, contact the group that interests you anyway—the organization is likely to at least send you some information and place you on a mailing list.

❑ PROGRAM DESCRIPTIONS

Once you've started to look at the individual listings, you'll find that they contain a lot of information. Naturally, there is a general description of the program(s), but wherever possible we have also included the following details.

Application Information

Each listing notes how far in advance you'll need to apply for the program or position, but the simple rule is to apply as far in advance as possible. This ensures that you won't miss out on a great opportunity simply because other people got there ahead of you. It also means that you will get a timely decision on your application, so if you are not accepted, you'll still have some time to apply elsewhere. As for the things that make up your application—essays, recommendations, etc.—we've tried to tell you what's involved, but be sure to contact the program about specific requirements before you submit anything.

Background Information

This includes such information as the date the program was established, the name of the organization that is sponsoring it, and the faculty and staff who will be there for you. This can help you—and your family—gauge the quality and reliability of the program. If we don't provide it here, be sure to get this information from the program itself.

Classes and Activities

Classes and activities change from year to year, depending on popularity, the availability of instructors, and many other factors. Nevertheless, colleges and universities quite consistently offer the same or similar classes, even in their summer sessions. Courses like Introduction to Journalism, Introduction to Health Care, or Introduction to Athletic Training, for example, are simply indispensable. So you can look through the listings and see which programs offer foundational courses like these and which offer courses on more variable topics. As for activities, we note when you have access to recreational facilities on campus, and it's a given that special social and cultural activities will be arranged for most programs.

Contact Information

Wherever possible, we have given the title of the person whom you should contact instead of the name because people change jobs so frequently. If no title is given and you are telephoning an organization, simply tell the person who answers the phone the name of the program or position that interests you and he or she will forward your call. If you are writing, include the line "Attention: Summer Baseball Camp" (or whatever is appropriate after "Attention") somewhere on the envelope. This will help to ensure that your letter goes to the person in charge of that program.

Credit

Where academic programs are concerned, we sometimes note that high school or college credit is available to those who have completed them. This means that the program can count toward your high school diploma or a future college degree just like a regular course. Obviously, this can be very useful, but it's important to note that rules about accepting such credit vary from school to school. Before you commit to a program offering high school credit, check with your guidance counselor to see if your school will grant you the credit. As for programs offering college credit, check with your chosen college (if you have one) to see if the institution will grant credit for the program.

Eligibility and Qualifications

These are difficult things to generalize. Some programs are very specific about their requirements—age, level of competition, etc.—while others accept all comers and sort them out by ability later. Get the details from the sponsoring organization and make sure you meet all the necessary qualifications before you send in your application or pay any registration fees.

Facilities

These may simply be sports facilities or, if the program is residential, they may include dormitory facilities as well. Knowing these kinds of details will help you set realistic expectations and determine whether you will be getting your money's worth.

Financial Details

Obviously, you need to know if there is a cost for your participation in the programs listed here and, if so, what that cost is. Prices do tend to go up each year, but they should be close to the figures we quote. Financial aid may be available for certain programs; simply ask before you apply.

Residential vs. Commuter Options

As a rule, residential programs are suitable for young people who live out of town or even out of state, as well as for local residents. Commuter programs may be viable only if you live near the program site or if you can stay with relatives who do. Internships are generally for commuters only. Bear in mind that for residential programs especially, the travel between your home and the location of the activity is almost always your responsibility and can significantly increase the cost of participation.

❏ FINALLY . . .

Ultimately, there are three important things to bear in mind concerning all of the programs listed in this volume. The first is that things change. Staff members come and go, funding is added or withdrawn, supply and demand determine which programs continue and which terminate. Dates, times, and costs vary widely because of a number of factors. Because of this, the information we give you, although as current and detailed as possible, is just not enough on which to base your final decision. If you are interested in a program, you simply must write, call, fax, or e-mail the organization in charge to get the latest and most complete information available. This has the added benefit of putting you in touch with someone who can deal with your individual questions and problems.

Another important point is that we do not recommend or endorse any of the programs or organizations listed in this book. The information given here comes from them, not from our own assessments. This is another reason for you to do your own research; once you get all the facts, you can judge all the merits of the programs for yourself.

The third thing to bear in mind is that the programs listed here are just the tip of the iceberg. There are links to other opportunities right in the "Surf the Web" and "Look to the Pros" chapters of section 4 in this book. But the bottom line is that no book can possibly cover all of the opportunities that are available to you—partly because they are so numerous and are constantly coming and going, and partly because some are still waiting to be discovered.

For instance, if you're interested in the baseball camp run by Jack Aker, but can't make it to any of the advertised locations, get in touch with a major- or minor-league team in your area and see if it runs a similar camp. Or perhaps you're interested in an internship with a basketball team but don't see one listed here. Phone the team and ask for the name of the person in charge of internships. You may then speak with that person on the phone or send a letter explaining your goals. In short, use the ideas behind these listings and take the initiative to turn them into opportunities!

❏ BASEBALL

Jack Aker Baseball
Camp/Clinic

Jack Aker spent 11 years in the major leagues as a pitcher, 10 as a manager, and 9 as a coach. The man knows baseball and now he works full-time, year-round as an instructor for amateur players. Aker works with people of all ages and has programs for both teams and individuals.

If you are currently on a team, you might ask your coach to investigate the possibility of having Jack Aker run a clinic for you. Clinics can run from a few hours to a few days, and prices start around $200. If you are part of a Native American community, it may be possible to arrange a special visit by Aker as part of the National Indian Youth Leadership Project; talk to a teacher or coach.

You can arrange private instruction with Jack Aker in New York or New Jersey or at one of his scheduled stops around the nation. Needless to say, this kind of instruction isn't cheap, but the prices seem reasonable, approximately $95 per hour. Aker also visits several summer camps each year; his Web site lists where you can meet up with him this summer. Contact Jack Aker Baseball for information on these and other programs.

Jack Aker Baseball
jackakerbaseball@aol.com
http://www.jackakerbaseball.com

❏ BASKETBALL
Sixers Camps
Camp/Clinic

If you want to be a professional basketball player in the future, doesn't it make sense to take instruction from those who are professional basketball players now? That's just what you can do at the official Philadelphia 76ers summer camps, which are taught by star NBA coaches and players. Boys ages 9 to 16 and girls ages 11 to 17 are welcome to attend one- or two-week residential sessions held in July and August. Costs range from about $585 to $1,275. All sessions are held in the Pocono Mountains, about two hours from both Philadelphia and New York City.

In addition, day camps are also offered in various locations in Delaware, New Jersey, and Pennsylvania. These camps teach participants the fundamentals of basketball, including ballhandling and dribbling, defense, offense, passing, shooting, and rebounding. Cost for the day camps is $340. Participants are required to provide their own transportation and lunch.

The Sixers will be happy to provide you with details on this year's sessions. If you have Internet access, look for a sample daily schedule and video clips from previous camps on their Web site. Whatever you do, do it early, because these camps fill up fast.

Sixers Camps
PO Box 1073
Bala Cynwyd, PA 19004-5073
610-668-7676
ask@sixerscamps.com
http://www.sixerscamps.com

❏ FIGURE SKATING
United States Figure Skating Association
Field Experience, Membership

Not surprisingly, the United States Figure Skating Association (USFSA) is the place to go for information on what is often called one of the world's most beautiful sports. Its Web site is particularly useful for the links to local figure skating clubs around America—in small communities as well as large. These clubs can help you get started in the sport and make new friends who share your interests. Of course, you can also get the information you want from the USFSA via mail, e-mail, or telephone!

United States Figure Skating Association
20 First Street
Colorado Springs, CO 80906-3624
719-635-5200
info@usfigureskating.org
http://www.usfsa.org

❏ FOOTBALL

Sports International Football Camps

Camp/Clinic

If you could choose anyone to help you improve your football game, you'd surely pick an NFL pro. Each Sports International Football Camp is taught by a pro; in choosing which camp you'll attend, you can actually choose which NFL player you'll be learning from. And, whether you choose Jay Novacek, Art Monk, Alex Brown, Antwaan Randle El, or another pro, you can expect him to bring along a few of his teammates as special guest instructors.

Boys ages 7 (accompanied by their father) to 18 are eligible to attend these camps, each of which lasts approximately one week. Costs range from $409 to $699. Specialty camps (based on posi-

tion) are also available. The best way to contact Sports International Football Camps is to get on the Internet, find out where each pro's camp will be located, and fill out the online form to request further information.

Sports International Football Camps
8924 McGaw Court
Columbia, MD 21045-4712
800-555-0801
http://www.footballcamps.com

❏ GOLF

American Junior Golf Association

Competition, Membership

The American Junior Golf Association (AJGA) is a nonprofit organization that is "dedicated to the overall growth and development of young men and women who aspire to earn college golf scholarships through competitive junior golf." Students ages 18 and younger are eligible for membership in the AJGA; membership fees range from $90 to $270 depending on membership level. The benefits of membership include a subscription to *Golfweek*, a newsletter, a copy of the current *United States Golf Association Rule Book*, a listing of national junior tournaments, and an annual college golf guide.

The AJGA sponsors several national tournaments for junior golfers between 13 and 18 who have succeeded at the state and local levels. Members of the American Junior Golf Association automatically receive applications for all non-invitational AJGA events. These tournaments often help players gain consideration for college golf scholarships.

American Junior Golf Association

1980 Sports Club Drive
Braselton, GA 30517-6000
877-373-2542
ajga@ajga.org
http://www.ajga.org

Ladies Professional Golf Association Girls Golf Club

Field Experience, Membership

The Ladies Professional Golf Association (LPGA) has sponsored the Girls Golf Club program since 1989. It started with just one club dedicated to getting young women involved in the sport and now offers the program at 181 locations throughout the country. Girls ages 7 to 17 are welcome to join the Girls Golf Club in their area to learn how to play golf in a fun and encouraging environment. The program's primary objective is to help you enjoy the game. Naturally, the LPGA Tour's current stars are involved in various ways with the Girls Golf Club program. For more information or to locate the Girls Golf Club in your area, contact the LPGA headquarters or browse their Web site.

Ladies Professional Golf Association Girls Golf Club

100 International Golf Drive
Daytona Beach, FL 32124-1092
386-274-6200
lpga.usgagirlsgolf@lpga.com
http://www.lpga.com/content_
    3.aspx?mid=7&pid=8

❏ HOCKEY
Planet Hockey
Camp/Clinic

Planet Hockey offers four- to five-day hockey camps at more than 50 locations throughout the United States and Canada. Program costs range from $289 to $395. The Planet Hockey Ranch, which is located in Breckenridge, Colorado, is a resident summer camp that provides hockey training along with adventure activities such as guided white-water rafting, mountain biking, biking, and more. The camp is typically held in June and July, and costs $1,199. Contact Planet Hockey for more information.

Planet Hockey

370 Cherokee Avenue
Superior, CO 80027-9693
800-320-7545
info@planethockey.com
http://www.planethockey.com

❏ SOCCER
Major League Soccer Camps
Camp/Clinic

Major League Soccer Camps is the official camp and clinic of Major League Soccer. MLS Camps offers more than 1,200 day camps each summer in 44 states. Two programs are available: the Play S.A.F.E. curriculum for younger, less-experienced players ages 4 through 10 and the A.T.T.A.C.K. curriculum for more experienced players ages 10 through 18. Those in the Play S.A.F.E. curriculum learn skills such as ball work, dribbling, passing and control, shooting, tackling and heading, teamwork, sportsmanship, goal setting, health and safety, and attacking, defending, types of possession, and decision making. Those in the A.T.T.A.C.K. curriculum learn the psychological components of competition, physical conditioning, tactical decision-making, rules of the game, and how to excel in highly competitive game settings. Contact Major League Soccer Camps for more information.

Major League Soccer Camps
800-284-6272
Helen.Castle@MLScamps.com
http://www.mlscamps.com

Northwestern Boys Soccer Academy

Camp/Clinic

Young men who are interested in soccer can participate in several summer programs at the Northwestern Boys Soccer Academy, which is held at Northwestern University in Evanston, Illinois. Four-day residential and commuter camps are available for boys in grades 4 through 10. Residential participants reside and eat their meals in university residence halls. Day camps are available to boys in grades one through eight. All camps are held at Northwestern's state-of-the-art indoor and outdoor facilities. Costs range from $175 to $525, depending on type of program. Applicants are strongly encouraged to apply before May 1 to be eligible for program discounts. The academy also offers a residential College Soccer Training Center for young men

ages 15 through 18 (including college freshman) who have advanced skills and hope to play in college. Costs for this four-day program range from $575 to $595. Contact the academy for further details.

Northwestern Boys Soccer Academy
PO Box 1822
Evanston, IL 60204-1822
847-491-9998
j-serpone@northwestern.edu
http://www.nusoccercamps.com/home.asp

❏ TENNIS

United States Tennis Association
Competition, Field Experience, Membership

The United States Tennis Association (USTA) is the organization that runs the U.S. Open Tennis Tournament, but it also manages other activities and competitions that encourage people of all ages to get involved in tennis. A membership in the USTA ($18 for those up to age 19) allows you to participate in a number of nationwide programs and competitions designed to help you develop your talents to the fullest. You may be particularly interested in USTA Junior Team Tennis, a round-robin league for boys and girls between the ages of 6 and 18; teams are organized according to age and skill. Your membership dues also entitle you to a subscription to *SMASH* magazine and admittance to tennis clubs around the country. Contact the United States Tennis Association for more details.

United States Tennis Association
http://www.usta.com

❏ VOLLEYBALL

United States Volleyball Association High Performance Program

Competition, Membership

If you play competitive volleyball, chances are you've already heard of USA Volleyball, which offers a variety of programs for those who have a love of and talent for volleyball. USA Volleyball's Junior Olympics offers indoor competitions and training for its members, separated by age. Junior Olympics events are conducted between October and June to allow junior players to supplement their interscholastic schedule. These events culminate in the Junior Olympic National Championships, a massive series of competitions lasting roughly one and a half weeks. Additionally, USA Volleyball's High Performance Program offers team and camp opportunities for boys and girls ages 13 through 18 who dream of representing the United States on the National Men's or Women's Volleyball Team. If you are interested in learning more, simply contact USA Volleyball for more information.

USA Volleyball
715 South Circle Drive
Colorado Springs, CO 80910-2306
719-228-6800
postmaster@usav.org
http://www.usavolleyball.org

❏ MULTIPLE-SPORT CAMPS

There are many camps and clinics around the United States and Canada that provide instruction in more than one sport. Most of these include some of the sports listed above as well as somewhat less-known sports. These programs are often run by colleges and prep schools, but also by independent operators. Don't be dismayed if your game isn't listed here. All sports are represented at some camp, somewhere—use summer camp reference books, the Internet, the telephone book, and the knowledge of your instructors to find the camp for you.

Nike Camps

Camp/Clinic

Sponsored by Nike and operated by US Sports Camps, these camps are open to all players who are serious about improving their particular game. Summer camps are available in baseball, basketball, field hockey, golf, lacrosse, running, softball, soccer, swimming, tennis, volleyball, and water polo. Camps are available throughout the United States. No matter where you attend camp, you'll play your particular sport all day, practicing various techniques and tactics, and you'll learn from professional coaches, who will provide a written evaluation of your play. Most sessions offer day, extended day, and resident options. Contact US Sports Camps for a brochure detailing this year's offerings.

US Sports Camps
4470 Redwood Highway
San Rafael, CA 94903

800-645-3226
http://us-sportscamps.com

Northern Michigan University
Camp/Clinic

The Northern Michigan University (NMU) Wildcats offer camps in basketball (separate camps for boys and girls), cross country, football, ice hockey, soccer, swimming and diving, and volleyball throughout June and July. Camps are open to young people in grades 3 through 12. Some camps differentiate between skills, conditioning, and varsity camps; check with NMU for details on your particular sport. Camps range in length from two to five days. Regardless of its focus, each camp is staffed by the Wildcats' own coaches and other collegiate coaches and athletes. Camps take place at facilities on the Northern Michigan University campus. At the completion of camp, all participants receive a written evaluation and a certificate of completion. The camps have residential and commuter options. Residents live on campus, eat in the cafeteria, and enjoy special evening recreation activities. Costs range between about $40 and $375 depending on sport and residency options. Application should be made at least three weeks prior to the start of camp; contact the NMU Athletic Department.

Northern Michigan University
Summer Sports Camps/Athletic
    Department
1401 Presque Isle Avenue
Marquette, MI 49855-5349
906-227-2519
http://newsbureau.nmu.edu/wildcats/
    camps.html

Sports and Arts Center at Island Lake
Camp/Clinic

The Sports and Arts Center at Island Lake offers training and/or competition in virtually every sport imaginable! Recent sports that were offered included archery, baseball, basketball, beach volleyball, bodybuilding, boxing, cheerleading, disc golf, fencing, field hockey, fitness, golf, karate, lacrosse, mountain boarding, roller hockey, soccer, softball, touch/flag football, volleyball, and wrestling. If all that isn't enough for you, remember that this is an arts center, too! There are many different courses in theater, dance, music, fine arts and crafts, and even magic and circus performing.

This is a residential camp with boys and girls staying on separate campuses in modern facilities. Island Lake has a fully equipped infirmary with six R.N.s and one physician in residence. Campers can stay for as little as two weeks or as long as eight weeks. Fees range from about $2,400 to $7,950 and are all inclusive. Except for transportation to and from the area, there are no extra costs—even your laundry is done for you. For more information on specific sports activities and other details, contact the Sports and Arts Center at Island Lake at the appropriate office or via the Internet.

**Sports and Arts Center at Island
    Lake**
Summer Office:
50 Island Lake Road
Starrucca, PA 18462-1069
570-798-2550
info@islandlake.com
http://www.islandlake.com

Winter Office:
136 East 57th Street, Suite 1001
New York, NY 10022-2965
800-869-6083
info@islandlake.com
http://www.islandlake.com

❏ ADDITIONAL OPPORTUNITIES

Those who are interested in pursuing opportunities in athletic training, or in sports-related fields such as broadcasting, journalism, health care, and management, will find the following resources of interest.

Athletic Training Summer Workshop at the University of Wisconsin–La Crosse

Camp/Clinic

High school students who are interested in a career in athletic training can participate in a one-day Athletic Training Summer Workshop at the University of Wisconsin–La Crosse (UWLC). Students learn about human anatomy, taping and wrapping techniques, the identification and treatment of sports injuries, emergency care and procedures, and sports nutrition and hydration via lectures and practical activities. The cost for this program is $80 (which includes a workshop manual, taping supplies, parking permits, and a workshop T-shirt). Applicants receive lunch, but are responsible for providing their own breakfast and dinner. The program is taught by certified athletic trainers, as well as students enrolled in the athletic training program at the university. Contact the Athletic Camps Office for more information.

Athletic Training Summer Workshop at the University of Wisconsin–La Crosse

Athletic Camps Office
25 Mitchell Hall
La Crosse, WI 54601
608-785-6544
http://www.uwlax.edu/AthleticTraining/athletictrainers06.pdf

Camp Chi

Camp/Clinic

Camp Chi, located near the beautiful Wisconsin Dells, features many activities in the fine arts, athletics, and outdoor adventure. Included in the arts category are radio and TV broadcasting. If you are interested in radio, for example, you will spend time at the camp's radio station, WCHI, learning all about radio broadcasting: how to operate the systems, interview talk-show guests, produce and direct shows, and be a DJ for your favorite music. After radio, you may choose to learn more about TV. Camp Chi has its own video studio where you can produce and direct TV shows, shoot and edit footage, and write scripts. TV and radio production is supervised by a staff member in that particular field.

In addition to all the activities, the camp, which is operated by the Jewish Community Centers of Chicago, has a heated swimming pool, a spring-fed lake with waterfront activities, a climbing and repelling wall, a roller hockey arena, rope courses, six tennis courts, and an animal farm. The staff-to-camper ratio is one to three. Camp Chi is for students ages 9 to 16. You stay in cabins with built-in bunk beds. If you're 14 to 16 years old, Camp Chi offers a separate village just for teens. Costs range from $1,050 to $3,995, depending on age level and program. This cost includes everything but transportation to the site. For an enrollment form, and to learn more about the camp, you can write, call, or e-mail. Visit Camp Chi's Web site, too.

Camp Chi
Summer Office:
PO Box 104
Lake Delton, WI 53940-0104
608-253-1681
info@campchi.com
http://www.campchi.com

Winter Office:
3050 Woodridge Road
Northbrook, IL 60062-7524
847-272-2301
info@campchi.com
http://www.campchi.com

College and Careers Program at the Rochester Institute of Technology

College Courses/Summer Study

The Rochester Institute of Technology (RIT) offers its College and Careers Program for rising seniors who want to experience college life and explore career options in business, science, and other subject areas. The program, founded in 1990, allows you to spend a Friday and Saturday on campus, living in the dorms and attending four sessions on the career areas of your choice. Sections that might be of interest to students who plan to pursue the business aspects of sports recently included Marketing: Will Your Idea Sell? and Management: Survivor, Business Style! Those interested in becoming sports physicians or trainers might find the following sections of interest: Computers in a Science or Pre-Med Track, Medical Ultrasound: Seeing Through Sound, Medical Sciences: Medical Detective—You Make the Call! Premedical Studies and Biomedical Sciences: What's Up Doc? and Premedical Studies: So, You Want to Be a Doctor? Those interested in becoming a sports statistician might want to sign up for "Mathematics & Statistics in the Real World." In each session, participants work with RIT students and faculty to gain hands-on experience in the subject area. This residential program is held twice each summer, usually once in mid-July and again in early August. The registration deadline is one week before the start of the program, but space is limited and students are accepted on a first-come, first-served basis. For further information about the program and specific sessions on offer, contact the RIT admissions office.

College and Careers Program
Rochester Institute of Technology
Office of Admissions
60 Lomb Memorial Drive
Rochester, NY 14623-5604
585-475-6631
https://ambassador.rit.edu/
    careers2006

Health Occupations Students of America (HOSA)

Competition, Conference, Membership

HOSA has been working since 1976 "to promote career opportunities in the health care industry and to enhance the delivery of quality health care to all people." It is an integral part of the health occupations curriculum in its member schools. The organization offers a range of competitions at the state and national levels. Qualifying HOSA participants compete in a variety of skill, leadership, and related events, including Biomedical Debate, CPR/First Aid, Emergency Medical Technician, First Aid/Rescue Breathing, Interviewing Skills, Job Seeking Skills, Medical Laboratory Assisting, Medical Math, Medical Terminology, Medical Spelling, Nursing Assisting, Practical Nursing, Personal Care, Physical Therapy, Speaking Skills, and Sports Medicine. HOSA also sponsors an annual national conference and also teams with a variety of organizations to offer scholarships. To participate in HOSA events, you must work through your school, so speak to a counselor or teacher about your interest in the organization.

Health Occupations Students of America
6021 Morriss Road, Suite 111
Flower Mound, TX 75028-3764
800-321-HOSA
http://www.hosa.org

High School Journalism Institute at Indiana University
College Courses/Summer Study
Rising high school sophomores, juniors, and seniors may participate in the High School Journalism Institute at Indiana University, a five-day residential or commuter program. Workshops are offered in Business/Advertising, Newspaper/News Magazine, Photojournalism, Television News, and Yearbook. Residential participants stay on separate floors (by gender) of Teter Residence Hall, which is air-conditioned and within walking distance of most workshop sessions. Cost for the five-day session for resident participants is $295; this includes tuition, residence hall room, and most supplies. Meal debit cards of either $40 or $70 are extra. Commuters pay $250 for the five-day session. Applications are typically due in June. Contact the institute for more information.

Indiana University
High School Journalism Institute
School of Journalism
940 East Seventh Street
Bloomington, IN 47405-7108
812-855-0895
ljjohnso@indiana.edu
http://www.journalism.indiana.edu/
  hsji/students.html

High School Summer Institute at Columbia College Chicago
College Courses/Summer Study
Rising high school sophomores, juniors, and seniors can take courses in 1 of 18 academic areas for college credit via Columbia's five-week High School Summer Institute. Academic areas of interest to readers of this book include Film and Video, Journalism, Radio, and Television. Recent classes included Creating a Television Program, News Reporting Basics, Introduction to Radio Broadcasting, and Introduction to Radio Sportscasting. All

courses are taught by regular Columbia College Chicago faculty, and most include field trips and hands-on experiences. Students who successfully complete their course(s) receive college credit from Columbia. Students stay in residence halls on campus; the approximately $1,400 room and board fee includes housing, an evening meal each day, and evening and weekend activities. Tuition is $150 per credit hour; there may be an additional charge for books and other materials. A limited number of scholarships are available. Contact the institute for further details.

High School Summer Institute
Columbia College Chicago
600 South Michigan Avenue
Chicago, IL 60605-1900
312-344-7130
summerinstitute@colum.edu
http://www2.colum.edu/admissions/
   hs_institute

International Radio and Television Society Foundation Inc.
Membership
This society is dedicated to keeping its members informed about the increasingly complex world of electronic media. Its student programs are primarily geared toward those at the college level, but high school students can join now to gain insight into the field of broadcasting. Most of the society's activities, such as its summer fellowship program and minority career workshop, take place in the New York area. As a student, you can join the International Radio and Television Soci-

ety under the "friend" membership category for about $50, a small price to pay to enjoy the benefits of this organization. Contact the society for more information on the benefits of membership.

International Radio and Television Society Foundation Inc.
420 Lexington Avenue, Suite 1601
New York, NY 10170-1602
212-867-6650
http://www.irts.org

Intern Exchange International Ltd.
Employment and Internship Opportunities
High school students ages 16 to 18 (including graduating seniors) who are interested in gaining real-life experience in business/finance, medicine, or public relations/marketing can participate in month-long summer internships in London, England. Participants work as interns in a variety of settings and gain hands-on experience by interacting with professionals in the field.

Month-long Career-Plus-Programmes in broadcasting and other fields are also available to high school students ages 16 to 18 (including graduating seniors). The program is held in London, England. Options are available in Print and Broadcast Journalism, Video Production, and other areas. Students learn about these fields via hands-on experience and workshop instruction.

The cost of either program is approximately $6,245, plus airfare; this fee includes tuition, housing (students live in residence halls at the University of London), breakfast and dinner daily, housekeeping service, linens and towels, special dinner events, weekend trips and excursions, group activities including scheduled theater, and a Tube Pass. Contact Intern Exchange International for more information.

Intern Exchange International Ltd.

2606 Bridgewood Circle
Boca Raton, FL 33434-4118
561-477-2434
info@internexchange.com
http://www.internexchange.com

Learning for Life Exploring Program

Field Experience

Learning for Life's Exploring Program is a career exploration program that allows young people to work closely with community organizations to learn life skills and explore careers. Opportunities are available in Business, Communications, Health, and other fields. Each Program has five areas of emphasis: Career Opportunities, Character Education, Leadership Experience, Life Skills, and Service Learning. As a participant in the Communications program, for example, you will work closely with reporters, producers, directors, and other radio and television professionals and learn about the demands and rewards of careers in the field.

To be eligible to participate in this programs, you must have completed the eighth grade and be 14 years old *or* be at least 15 years of age but have not reached your twenty-first birthday. This program is open to both males and females.

To find a Learning for Life office in your area (there are more than 300 located throughout the United States), contact the Learning for Life Exploring Program.

Learning for Life Exploring Program

1325 West Walnut Hill Lane,
   PO Box 152079
Irving, TX 75015-2079
972-580-2433
http://www.learningforlife.org/
   exploring/communications/index.
   html

Medical Application of Science and Health at the Southwest Louisiana Area Health Education Center

Camp/Clinic

The Southwest Louisiana Area Health Education Center sponsors an annual Medical Application of Science and Health program—known as M*A*S*H—to students entering 10th through 12th grades. This two-week program serves to orient students on different career paths in the health care industry. M*A*S*H students learn how to read throat cultures, conduct EKGs, study college-level biology, take medical technology classes, and meet one-on-one with doctors from a range of specialties. After successful completion of the program and exam, students earn three or four hours of college credit. To be eligible, applicants must have at least a 3.4 GPA on a 4.0 scale. The program is offered at the University of Louisiana–

Lafayette and McNeese State University. Visit the organization's Web site for more information on the program.

If this camp sounds interesting, but you don't live in Louisiana, visit the National Area Health Education Center Organization's Web site, http://www. nationalahec.org/home/index.asp, to see if similar programs are available in your state.

Southwest Louisiana Area Health Education Center

Medical Application of Science and
  Health Program
103 Independence Boulevard
Lafayette, LA 70506-6086
800-435-2432
careers@swlahec.com
http://www.swlahec.com/index.
  php?option=com_content&task=vi
  ew&id=103&Itemid=142

SkillsUSA

Competition

SkillsUSA offers "local, state and national competitions in which students demonstrate occupational and leadership skills." Students who participate in its SkillsUSA Championships can compete in categories such as 3-D Visualization and Animation, Basic Health Care Skills, Customer Service, Electronics Applications, Electronics Technology, First Aid/CPR, Health Knowledge Bowl, Health Occupations Professional Portfolio, Photography, and Television (Video) Production. SkillsUSA works through high schools and colleges rather than directly with studetns, so ask your guidance counselor or teacher if it

is an option for you. Visit the SkillsUSA Web site for more information.

SkillsUSA

PO Box 3000
Leesburg, VA 20177-0300
703-777-8810
http://www.skillsusa.org

Summer Youth Programs at Michigan Technological University

College Courses/Summer Study

Michigan Technological University offers the Summer Youth Program for students in grades 6 through 11. Participants attend one of four weeklong sessions usually held during the months of July or August, choosing either to commute or to live on campus. Students undertake an "exploration" in one of many career fields through field trips and discussions with MTU faculty and other professionals. Classes recently offered included Careers in Health and Fitness, Creative Writing, Finance, Introduction to Business, Medical Physiology, Microbiology, and Photography. The cost of the Summer Youth Program is approximately $525 for the residential option, $325 for commuters. Applications are accepted up to one week before the program begins.

Michigan Technological University

Summer Youth Program
Youth Programs Office, Alumni
  House
1400 Townsend Drive
Houghton, MI 49931-1295
906-487-2219
http://youthprograms.mtu.edu

United States Association for Blind Athletes

Camp/Clinic, Membership

The association assists blind or visually impaired athletes in the United States. Visit its Web site for information on sports camps and the National Sports Education Camps Project. Young people age 21 and under who are blind or visually impaired may also become junior members for a fee of $25.

United States Association for Blind Athletes
33 North Institute Street
Colorado Springs, CO 80903-3508
719-630-0422
http://www.usaba.org

Women's Sports Foundation

Employment and Internship Opportunities, Membership

The Women's Sports Foundation is a nonprofit organization founded in 1974 by Billie Jean King to ensure gender equality and promote female participation in sports. Anyone with an interest in women's sports can become a member of the foundation (the cost is usually $30, but those 13 and under pay only $20), which welcomes student help. Paid internships are reserved for college students, but volunteerships are available for high school students who live in the area. Contact the Educational Services Coordinator about volunteering, or visit the foundation's Web site to learn more.

Women's Sports Foundation
Attn: Educational Services
    Coordinator
Eisenhower Park
East Meadow, NY 11554
800-227-3988
info@womenssportsfoundation.org
http://www.womenssportsfoundation.
    org/cgi-bin/iowa/index.html

Read a Book

When it comes to finding out about sports, don't underestimate books. (You're reading one now, after all.) What follows is a short, annotated list of books and periodicals related to sports. The books range from fiction to personal accounts of what it's like to be a professional athlete, to professional volumes on specific topics, such as sports medicine. Don't be afraid to check out the professional journals, either. The technical stuff may be way above your head right now, but if you take the time to become familiar with one or two, you're bound to pick up some of what is important to sports personnel, not to mention begin to feel like a part of their world— which is what you're interested in, right?

We've tried to include recent materials as well as old favorites. Always check for the most recent editions, and, if you find an author you like, ask your librarian to help you find more. Keep reading good books!

Note: In addition to those titles listed here, there are magazines that concentrate on every specific sport. Check the listings in the Sports section of *Magazines for Libraries,* 14th ed. (New York: Bowker, 2004), for recommended titles.

❏ BOOKS

Andrews, Phil. *All American Sports IQ Test: Ultimate Playbook of Trivia, Teasers and Puzzles.* New York: Sporting News Books, 2004. Features challenging trivia and other challenges for sports fanatics.

———. *Sports Journalism: A Practical Introduction.* Thousand Oaks, Calif.: Sage, 2005. This book provides an overview of broadcast, print, and digital sports media and offers tips on conducting interviews, covering sports events, and writing news stories, features, and profiles.

Ashe, Arthur, and Arnold Rampersad. *Days of Grace: A Memoir*. New York: Random House, 1994. The great tennis pro tells of his experiences with racism, his tireless crusade for justice, and his last tough battle with AIDS.

Baine, Celeste. *High Tech Hot Shots: Careers in Sports Engineering.* Alexandria, Va.: National Society of Professional Engineers, 2004. Profiling more than 20 potential career opportunities for students with an aptitude for math and science, this book demonstrates how to take a love of sports and fitness and to combine it with an engineering degree in order to work as a sports engineer. You'll learn about everything from working as an engineer in extreme sports such as skateboarding and snowboarding to building stadiums or designing sports equipment.

Birrer, Richard B. *Sports Medicine for the Primary Care Physician.* 3d ed. Boca Raton, Fla.: CRC Press, 2004. This book addresses topics in sports science/medicine that affect primary care physicians.

Boston Globe. *Greatness: The Rise of Tom Brady.* Chicago: Triumph Books, 2005. This book profiles star NFL quarterback Tom Brady.

Buren, Jodi. *Superwomen: 100 Women–100 Sports.* New York: Bulfinch Press, 2004. This inspiring book celebrates women in sports—from well-known superstars to those who have overcome mental and physical disabilities—via photographs and comments from the athletes.

Crutcher, Chris. *Athletic Shorts: Six Short Stories.* New York: HarperTempest, 2002. These fictional accounts of young athletes written for young adults tackle racism, homophobia, sexism, and growing up.

———. *Running Loose.* New York: HarperTempest, 2003. Louie Banks's love of football is challenged by his encounter with an unethical coach in this novel by an author whose trademark is combining fast-paced sports action with personal development in the teenage years.

Dickson, Paul. *The Joy of Keeping Score: How Scoring the Game Has Influenced and Enhanced the History of Baseball.* New York: Walker, 1996. A quirky look at a little-known side of baseball with surprising insights into how scoring techniques have affected how the game is played.

Freeman, Michael. *ESPN: The Uncensored History.* Lanham, Md.: Taylor Trade, 2002. Provides an in-depth look at the founding and growth of cable sports giant ESPN.

Halberstam, David. *The Education of a Coach.* New York: Hyperion, 2005. Pulitzer-winning journalist David Halberstam profiles top NFL coach Bill Belichick in this engaging book.

Heitzmann, William Ray, and Mark Rowh. *Careers for Sports Nuts & Other Athletic Types.* New York: McGraw-Hill, 2004. Offering advice to the individual who wants to work in the sports industry, the authors of this volume of the Careers for You Series discuss the skills, education, and training needed to land that dream job in sports.

Jackson, Phil, and Hugh Delehanty. *Sacred Hoops: Spiritual Lessons of a Hardwood Warrior.* New York: Hyperion, 1995. An earnest and refreshing look at pro basketball from the man who has coached Michael Jordan and the Chicago Bulls to championship seasons.

Kilduff, Mike. *The Passion for Sports: Athletes Tell Their Stories of Why They Love Their Games.* New York: Sporting News Books, 2002. Star athletes—such as Curt Schilling, George Brett, Kobe Bryant, Elton Brand, Emmitt Smith, Peyton and Eli Manning, Mario Lemieux, Mario Andretti, and Kevin Harvick—detail their love of their respective sports.

Kinsella, W. P. *Shoeless Joe.* Boston: Houghton Mifflin, 1999. A fan builds a baseball stadium for a legendary game with Shoeless Joe Jackson and other baseball immortals. A classic sports story.

Kristy, Davida. *Coubertin's Olympics: How the Games Began*. Minneapolis: Lerner, 1995. Fascinating account of Baron Pierre De Coubertin, the man whose vision and tenacity led to the founding of the modern Olympic movement in 1896.

Levy, Marilyn. *Run for Your Life*. New York: Penguin, 1997. While living in a housing project in Oakland, California, 13-year-old Kisha joins a track team that helps her discover she has the ability to become a winner in this fast-paced novel.

Lupica, Mike (ed.). *The Best American Sports Writing 2005*. Boston: Houghton Mifflin, 2005. This book presents the best in sportswriting, profiling well-known sports, teams, and athletes, as well as those competing joyfully on the fringes of competition.

Miller, Ernestine. *Making Her Mark: Firsts and Milestones in Women's Sports*. New York: McGraw-Hill, 2002. This fascinating book chronicles the rise of women's sports from the 1880s to the present.

O'Connor, Francis G., et al. *Sports Medicine: Just the Facts*. New York: McGraw-Hill Professional, 2004. Provides a concise overview of diagnostic and treatment procedures for sports physicians.

Phillips, Dave, and Rob Rains. *Center Field on Fire: An Umpire's Life With Pine Tar Bats, Spitballs, and Corked Personalities*. Chicago: Triumph Books, 2003. This memoir, written by a professional baseball umpire (Phillips), recounts behind-the-scenes experiences from the usual daily routine in the life of an umpire to the wild situations that sometimes occur on the diamond.

Schlachter, Gail A., and David R. Weber. *College Student's Guide to Merit and Other No-Need Fund*ing. El Dorado Hills, Calif.: Reference Service Press, 2005. This directory for students who are currently enrolled in college references over 1,200 sources of available funding for those who might believe they are not eligible for financial aid. No set income level is required for any of the listings in this book—they are based solely on a student's ability in a subject matter, athletic success, religious or ethnic background, and much more.

Staten, Vince. *Why Is The Foul Pole Fair? Answers to 101 of the Most Perplexing Baseball Questions*. New York: Simon & Schuster, 2004. This book provides an in-depth, but humorous, look at the entertaining, yet sometimes confusing, world of baseball.

Tibballs, Geoff. *The Olympics' Strangest Moments: Extraordinary But True Tales From The History Of The Olympic Games*. London, U.K.: Robson Books, 2005. Full of unusual and hard-to-believe tales from the Olympic Games, this book provides sports lovers with a unique account of some of the strangest occurrences in Olympic Games history.

United States Tennis Association. *Coaching Tennis Successfully*. 2d ed. Champaign, Ill.: Human Kinetics, 2004. This book features practical advice on coaching tennis from coaches at the high school through professional levels.

Wilson, Robert F. *Careers in Sports, Fitness, and Recreation.* Hauppauge, N.Y.: Barron's Educational Series, 2001. As part of the Success Without College series, this book highlights well-paying and rewarding careers in sports that do not require a college degree. Most of the jobs featured, including refereeing, umpiring, sports club management, or equipment sales, do require some level of professional training.

❏ PERIODICALS

Athletic Business. Published monthly by Athletic Business Publications Inc. (4130 Lien Road, Madison, Wis. 53704-3602, 800-722-8764, circ@ athleticbusiness.com, http://www.athleticbusiness.com). Containing articles of interest to individuals responsible for the business of planning, financing, marketing, and operating of athletic and fitness facilities, this publication features columns on sports law, high school and college sports, military and recreation, and more.

Current Sports Medicine Reports. Published bimonthly by the American College of Sports Medicine (PO Box 1440, Indianapolis, Ind. 46206-1440, 800-638-3030, http://www.acsm.org/publications/csmr.htm), this physician-reviewed journal offers reviews of the most current medical literature in the major sports medicine categories.

Health & Fitness Journal. Published bimonthly by the American College of Sports Medicine (PO Box 1440, Indianapolis, Ind. 46206-1440, 800-638-3030, http://www.acsm-healthfitness.org), this online journal contains articles of interest to health and fitness professionals such as personal trainers and fitness instructors. Product developments and trends in the industry are the publication's focus.

International Gymnast. Published monthly by Paul Ziert and Associates (PO Box 721617, Norman, Okla. 73070-8240, 800-664-5266, subscriptions@intlgymnast.com, http://www.intlgymnast.com). Providing an inside look at gymnastics competitions and events throughout the world, this magazine contains profiles, interviews, and training information in the world of gymnastics.

Journal of Applied Sport Psychology. Published quarterly by Taylor and Francis Inc. (325 Chestnut Street, Suite 800, Philadelphia, Pa. 19106-2608, 800-354-1420, http://www.aaasponline.org/publications.php), this peer-reviewed journal of the Association for the Advancement of Applied Sport Psychology contains articles on the latest research in the field of sport psychology.

Journal of Physical Education, Recreation, and Dance. Published monthly by the American Alliance for Health, Physical Education, Recreation and

Dance (1900 Association Drive, Reston, Va. 20191-1502, 703-476-3400, http://www.aahperd.org/aahperd/template.cfm?template=publications.html), this industry journal contains diverse articles on topics of interest to professionals who "are committed to improving the quality of life through the movement arts and sciences, sport, and leisure." Recent issues have included articles on teaching strategies, ethics and gender equality in sports, and leisure for older adults.

Journal of Sport History. Published three times a year by the North American Society for Sport History (Subscriptions, PO Box 1026, Lemont, Pa. 16851-1026, secretary-treasurer@nassh.org, http://www.nassh.org/index1.html). For the true sports history buff, this publication contains detailed scholarly articles and lengthy book reviews that offer a fascinating historical perspective on sports.

Journal of Sport Management. Published quarterly by the North American Society for Sport Management (Business Office, West Gym 014, Slippery Rock University, Slippery Rock, Pa. 16057, 800-321-0789, naspe@aahperd.org, http://www.nassm.com/InfoAbout/JSM), this professional journal for industry insiders features research studies and articles on a wide variety of topics relating to sport and exercise.

Medicine & Science in Sports & Exercise. Published monthly by the American College of Sports Medicine (PO Box 1440, Indianapolis, Ind. 46206-1440, 800-638-3030, http://www.acsm-msse.org), this multidisciplinary scholarly journal includes features, clinical studies, and reviews of interest to a wide range of professionals in fields such as exercise physiology, physical therapy, medicine, athletic training, and more.

Olympic Review: Official Publication of the Olympic Movement. Published monthly by the Olympic Studies Centre (Quai d'Ouchy 1, PO Box 1001, Lausanne, Switzerland, http://www.olympic.org/uk/news/search/index_uk.asp?prov=review), this firsthand view of the international Olympic scene has been the official publication of the Olympic Movement since 1894.

Referee. Published monthly by Referee Enterprises (2017 Lathrop Avenue, Racine, Wisc. 53405-3758, 800-733-6100, cservice@referee.com, http://www.referee.com), this magazine, dedicated to sports officiating, covers a wide range of topics including the psychology and legal aspects of refereeing. Each issue contains interviews, personality profiles, investigative reports, and feature articles.

The Sporting News. Published weekly, (800-777-6785, http://www.sporting-news.com), this publication provides extensive coverage of football, baseball, hockey, basketball, and other sports.

Sport Marketing Quarterly. Published quarterly by West Virginia University

(PO Box 6116, Morgantown, W.Va. 26506-6116, 800-477-4348, http://www.smqonline.com), this research-oriented journal caters to sports marketing professionals. Each issue contains articles and reports on sport marketing and law, case studies, and profiles and interviews.

The Sport Psychologist. Published quarterly by Human Kinetics Publishers (Subscriptions, PO Box 5076, Champaign, Ill. 61825-5076, 800-747-4457, info@hkusa.com, http://www.humankinetics.com/TSP/journalAbout.cfm), this scholarly journal contains articles on applied research and professional practice; profiles; and book and resource reviews.

Sports Business Journal. Published weekly by Street and Smith's Sports Group (Subscriptions, 120 West Morehead Street, Suite 310, Charlotte, N.C. 28202-1826, 800-829-9839, http://www.sportsbusinessjournal.com). Targeted to business executives in the sports industry, this publication provides news and features covering deals, trades, and contracts. All business areas of the sports industry are covered.

Sport Scene. Published quarterly by North American Youth Sport Institute (Subscriptions, PO Box 957, Kernersville, N.C. 27285-0957, 336-784-4926, http://www.naysi.com/sport_scene/sport_scene.htm), this magazine, targeted to parents, teachers, and children's sporting league professionals, contains articles on how to make sports fun for children while educating them about lifelong fitness and health.

Sports Illustrated. Published weekly by Time Warner (Subscriptions, PO Box 30602, Tampa, Fla. 33630-0602, 800-528-5000, http://sportsillustrated.cnn.com), this well-known magazine provides timely, informative articles, with great photography, on every aspect of the sports industry. It highlights outstanding professional, college, and amateur athletes in football, basketball, baseball, soccer, the Olympics, and more.

Strategies: A Journal for Physical and Sport Educators. Published bimonthly by the American Alliance for Health, Physical Education, Recreation and Dance (1900 Association Drive, Reston, Va. 20191-1502, 703-476-3400, http://www.aahperd.org/naspe/template.cfm?template=strategies_main.html), this peer-reviewed magazine features articles of interest to physical education professionals who work with children of all ages.

Training & Conditioning. Published nine times per year by Momentum Media (Subscriptions, PO Box 4806, Ithaca, N.Y. 14852-4806, 607-257-6970, http://www.momentummedia.com/tc.htm), this trade publication for sports medicine and fitness professionals contains feature articles and news updates of interest to those who train competitive athletes.

Women in Sport and Physical Activity Journal. Published biannually online by the National Association for Girls & Women in Sport (1900 Association Drive, Reston, Va. 20191-1502, 703-476-3400, http://www.aahperd.org/ wspaj), this peer-reviewed, scholarly online journal covers sports and physical fitness as they pertain to women. Issues include research-based articles, reviews, commentary, and more.

Surf the Web

You must use the Internet to do research, to find out, and to explore. The Internet is the closest you'll get to what's happening right now all around the world. This chapter gets you started with an annotated list of Web sites related to sports. Try a few. Follow the links. Maybe even venture as far as asking questions in a chat room. The more you read about and interact with sports personnel, the better prepared you'll be when you're old enough to participate as a professional.

One caveat: You probably already know that URLs change all the time. If a Web address listed below is out of date, try searching on the site's name or other key words. Chances are, if it's still out there, you'll find it. If it's not, maybe you'll find something better!

About.com: Radio
http://home.about.com/sports

About.com tells you everything you want to know "about" any given subject. The sports page, therefore, covers everything sports—from the most recent national or world sports headlines to suggested reading about choosing a surfboard. The main sports categories appear on the left-hand side of the page, and with each click of the button, you delve deeper into the subject. Spectator sports, hunting/fishing, marine, and fitness/outdoor are your

most broad choices. Choose any subheading and you'll find a list of recent articles that have been published on the topic—usually within the last two weeks. Each click of the mouse narrows your search even further. Articles are provided free of charge, which means that you can expect to find plenty of advertisements and links to related online shopping sites.

American College of Sports Medicine (ACSM)
http://www.acsm.org//AM/Template. cfm?Section=Home_Page

The American College of Sports Medicine's Web site provides a glimpse into the field of sports medicine. This field of medicine, it turns out, is as much about getting the average person to get up off the couch as it is about performing laser surgery on a superstar athlete's knee. A good example is the college's involvement with the U.S. Department of Health's Healthy People 2010 initiative. You can read online about the specific physical activity and fitness objectives that the American College of Sports Medicine (ACSM) is working to implement. There's also a decent introductory section about the ACSM itself. What started as a group of 11 physicians, physiologists, and educators back in 1954 has evolved into an organization with more than

20,000 members in professions such as cardiology, exercise physiology, nutrition, personal training, health club directing, professional and amateur team medicine, and research. The group holds an annual meeting where research studies and workshops are presented. You can also read a bit about the ACSM's professional publications, which include the journals *Medicine and Science in Sports and Exercise, Exercise and Sport Sciences Reviews,* and *ACSM's Health & Fitness Journal.* Perhaps of greatest interest are the materials that can be requested by the general public, which include the brochures *Careers in Sports Medicine and Exercise Science,* and *Nutrition and Sports Performance: A Guide for Physically Active Young People.*

Associated Press Sports Editors
http://apse.dallasnews.com

This is the official Web site of the Associated Press Sports Editors, a membership organization that strives to improve print journalistic standards in sports newsrooms. Web site visitors will find up-to-date news articles regarding industry happenings, a job board, and a downloadable monthly newsletter, as well as links to all of the major sports Web sites for professional sports organizations and leagues. Membership information, including an in-depth profile of the organization, is also included.

CampSearch
http://www.campsearch.com

CampSearch is an excellent search engine that sorts through more than 2,000 camps.

The home page organizes camps into the following categories: overnight, day, residential, specialty, tours and adventures, focused, outdoor education, and family. To get a comprehensive list of camps that are tailor-made for you, just do a keyword search according to the activities you want to do (such as baseball, tennis, snowboarding, or golf). Or construct your search according to special needs or geographic locations. If you (or your parents) don't want to foot the bill, then maybe the CampJobs Network (on CampSearch's home page) should be the next click of your mouse. Here you'll find various paid positions that will at least put you to work in a sporting environment.

ESPN SportsZone
http://espn.go.com

When it comes to sportscasting, ESPN is head and shoulders above the competition—on the Web as well as on TV. This site covers baseball, football, hockey, soccer, golf, basketball, auto racing, tennis, and more. It is dynamic and easy to navigate, with a column on the left-hand side of the page listing each sport ESPN covers in detail, as well as fantasy sports. Also listed are resources such as ESPN wireless, podcasts, and a searchable database of leagues and sporting activities to join. Once you've finished checking the latest scores, click on Join Our Team for actual career-related information. At any given time ESPN Studios may list a vast range of job titles including event production coordinator, associate producer, and media associate. You can even fill out and send an application online. Students may also spend some time reviewing the college relations section to learn about and apply for internship opportunities with ESPN.

Gatorade Sports Science Institute

http://www.gssiweb.com

Thinking about becoming an athletic trainer, physician, or coach? Then you'll want to start learning about sports medicine, sports nutrition, and exercise science. Surprisingly enough, Gatorade Sports Science Institute's site is much more than just a plug for Gatorade drinks. It's full of valuable information and articles. Most of the material of interest here falls under the Sports Science Library. In this section, you can read a variety of articles and discussions by experts in exercise science and sports medicine. You'll find plenty of practical information on dietary supplements, environmental conditions and sports training, hydration, sports nutrition, and sports psychology.

The Hockey News

http://www.thn.com/en/home/home. asp

If you follow hockey at all, you probably already know that this is one of the foremost periodicals covering the sport. Both old and new readers should find this Web site informative and useful. Once you've finished perusing this week's online edition of the magazine, take a look at *The Hockey News'* Hockey School Guide. This is a great resource for American and Canadian players alike, allowing you to search more than 120 summer hockey schools

and camps by geographic area. The listings give you all the basic information you need: location, contact information, dates and times, age groups, sleeping and entertainment facilities, and specialized programs. Female hockey players will be pleased to find camps for both males and females.

Hockeyweekly.com

http://www.hockeyweekly.com

It's an unavoidable fact that if you want to play a sport professionally, you first have to spend some time as an amateur. If hockey is the sport you love, then Hockey Weekly can help you make the most of your amateur days. This subscription site offers news articles and an online guide to hockey schools and listings of leagues and tournaments, as well as sections on less common topics such as roller hockey. In order to access full articles and information on high school leagues, college leagues, junior leagues, AAA leagues, local leagues, and tryout postings for all of these, you'll need to subscribe. Register online to receive a free newsletter.

Major League Baseball

http://mlb.mlb.com/NASApp/mlb/ index.jsp

Every National League and American League team is represented on this all-encompassing baseball Web site. The most up-to-date scoop on who's been traded, the day's real-time baseball scores from across the country, and links to purchasing tickets to games in cities across the United States can be accessed on this baseball lover's must-bookmark site.

You'll also find headlines, news, and video clips along with editorials, complete stats, and the ultimate fantasy forum. Message boards, live chats, and blogs keep fans connected to their peers. You may also choose to register for free newsletters and e-mail updates if you want to make reading each day's baseball news part of your daily inbox routine.

Major League Soccer
http://www.mlsnet.com/MLS/index.jsp

Check out the Official Site for Major League Soccer and discover everything you ever wanted to know about this increasingly popular sport in the United States. You'll find all the latest news, schedules, scores, stats, standings, team information, and player bios for the 12 Eastern and Western Conference teams. Purchase tickets, shop online, or find updates on new soccer-related competitions or events. If you're a novice soccer fan, you can also catch up on the history of the league or the rules of the game. Parents and kids should also check out the information to learn about youth soccer leagues. Job seekers will find multiple postings for sports personnel positions across the country.

National Athletic Trainers' Association
http://www.nata.org

Looking for career information about the field of athletic training? You've come to the right place. For starters, read about what an athletic trainer does and discover everything about the past, present, and future of the field. You'll discover what a typical day might include, the education and extra training that may be required, and where you could eventually work. The National Athletic Trainers Association (NATA) is a nonprofit organization committed to the advancement, encouragement, and improvement of the athletic training profession. So committed, in fact, that the NATA will even help some students pay for their college education. The organization's foundation distributes 70 scholarships annually to college students and also funds various grants and awards. If you're in the process of choosing a college, there's also some great information here about which universities have accredited athletic training education programs for undergraduates.

National Basketball Association
http://www.nba.com

This official site of the National Basketball Association (NBA) has everything a seasoned basketball fan craves—up-to-the minute scoreboards, news, standings, and fantasy league stats. You can even listen and watch games live via this site. Interested in the business of basketball? You can read all about the latest contract talks, negotiations, and transactions. But this site contains far more than just NBA team updates; you'll also discover links to the Developmental League, the Women's National Basketball Association, and global teams. Television schedules of game coverage are also listed, or you can sign up to receive score updates on your cell phone. Register to receive a free newsletter, screen savers, games, and more.

National Collegiate Athletic Association (NCAA)

http://www.ncaa.org

This is an exemplary site; it's visually appealing and divides masses of information about college athletics into manageable sections. If you're on the way to playing college sports—or even if you're just a fan—this site might become one of your favorites. The Initial-Eligibility Clearinghouse is specifically for the college-bound athlete. It's loaded with information to help parents and student-athletes understand the initial eligibility requirements for Division I and II schools. It also answers many of the frequently asked questions about the recruiting process. The NCAA School and Conference Athletic Web sites section breaks schools into Division I, II, and III schools. Both of these sections contain tons of information that student athletes will find important.

Here's a quick rundown of what else you'll find at this site. Under General Information, you'll get the history of the NCAA and get a feel for its programs, services, scholarships, special events, and job listings. The Media and Events section offers publications and videos covering rules, statistics, sports sciences, research, and records. In Sports & Championships, you can check out the sites of NCAA championships and find links to each sport's championship page. Finally, the Statistics section has—no surprises here—weekly statistics on football, women's volleyball, men's and women's basketball, baseball, softball, men's and women's lacrosse, and men's ice hockey.

National Football League (NFL)

http://www.nfl.com

The NFL's official Web site features icons for each of the teams running along the top of the opening page (where you can easily link to their home pages for team-specific info). The league's site is divided into eleven major categories: Depth Charts, News, NFL Shop, Players, Rosters, Schedules, Scores, Standings, Statistics, Teams, and Players. Go into the News section to read what's essentially an online version of a newspaper's sports pages. (If only your newspaper were so single-minded about professional football!) The rest of the sections are pretty self-explanatory. No matter what your chosen career is—recruiter, agent, coach, player, sports marketer—this site can keep you primed on what's happening in football. Links to team and league employment are also available. Naturally, you're getting the NFL's party line about anything controversial here, but you're also getting reliable information and prompt updates.

Olympic.org

http://www.olympic.org/uk/index_ uk.asp

Whether you're a fan of Olympic sports or an amateur athlete yourself who dreams of one day having your picture on this Web site, this official site of the Olympic Movement profiles athletes and contains the latest news on recent competitions. You'll also find a complete history of Olympic sports, as well as current lists of all recognized sports. Check out the Media Centre for the latest athlete news and more. View the organizational chart of the organization, research its history, and discover what is meant by Olympic passion. This Web site also lists job opportunities that are available with this prestigious organization.

Peterson's Education Portal

http://www.petersons.com

This site offers anything you want to know about surviving high school, getting into college, and choosing a graduate degree. Check out the College and Graduate School sections, which offer school directories searchable by key word, degree, location, tuition, size, GPA, and even sports offered. This site is not devoted to athletic-related schools, but it is worthy of a visit for its comprehensiveness; school listings offer the usual basics plus details on financial aid, school facilities, student government, faculty, and admissions requirements.

Peterson's Guide to Summer Programs for Teenagers

http://www.petersons.com/
summerop

This Web site provides great information on sports-focused summer programs. Finding a camp that suits your interests is easy enough at this site; just search Peterson's database of sports programs. Under the Sports heading, you'll find a list of links to more than 100 activities, from basketball to climbing to kayaking to squash—to name a few. Click on a topic and then a specific program or camp for a quick overview description. In some instances you'll get a more in-depth description, along with photographs,

applications, and online brochures. If you need to limit your search to your home state, that's easy enough, too. You can sift through Peterson's database geographically or alphabetically.

Princeton Review

http://www.princetonreview.com/
home.asp

Similar to the Peterson's Web site, Princeton Review is a great site to find comprehensive college reviews and information. Unique to this site are actual student comments about each school, which offer refreshingly honest opinions about the institution and its student body. Check out the site's annual rankings to read how schools stack up in academics, social scene, diversity, and other areas. Under the Students Tell All section, read about what students have to say about their college experience.

Professional Golf Association (PGA) Online

http://www.pga.com/home

This is a friendly site that reflects golf's savvy (and successful) efforts to draw new players and fans to the sport. The Juniors section is really a site unto itself. There's a page that covers etiquette on the course, another page that has a summary of the rules of golf, one about the PGA's new introductory lessons called First Swing, and several other informative and well-written pages. Elsewhere in PGA Online, you'll find a section called Improve Your Game. This site is for those who are already hooked on golf and who need to improve their technique. Visitors can learn how to shift their weight, improve their grip, and choose a putter. There's plenty to keep you busy at this Web site. For instance, if you want to take a trip to a PGA event, you can book your travel here. Or delve into the PGA of America section, which is an excellent resource for those who want to become pros. If that's your goal, you'll find information on the steps to take as well as employment opportunities.

Special Olympics

http://www.specialolympics.org/
   Special+Olympics+Public+Website/
   default.htm

This international nonprofit organization's Web site highlights competitions and event calendars as well as numerous ways to get involved with this highly regarded organization that is "dedicated to empowering individuals with intellectual disabilities to become physically fit, productive, and respected members of society through sports training and competition." Visit this Web site if you or someone you love qualifies to register for competitions or if you are interested in coaching, volunteering, or seeking employment with this organization. Interested in finding out more about this organization? You'll find a downloadable annual report at this Web site, as well a link to subscribe, free of charge, to the organization's official magazine, *Spirit*.

SportsKnowHow.com

http://www.sportsknowhow.com

Are you a detail-oriented person? Organizing your own sports league? Want to impress someone with your knowledge of the rules of baseball? Interested in constructing your own regulation-sized shuffleboard court? This Web site provides everything you need to know about court and field dimensions, rules, and "how-to" information galore for sports from bocce to badminton, pickleball to horseshoes. If you've never heard of some of these sports, you'll want to visit this educational and informative Web site. And it might just help you win a game or two of Trivial Pursuit!

Yahoo: Recreation: Sports

http://dir.yahoo.com/Recreation/Sports

This popular search engine provides an A to Z database of sports-related categories. You'll find thousands of links to sports and related topics, which may be overwhelming. But if you're looking for hard-to-find details on topics such as sports mascots, sports officiating, or stadiums and venues, you'll find this search engine a most helpful source of information. The site divides its database into two categories—types of sports and sporting resources. This is an excellent first-stop Web site if you are researching a sport-related topic and don't know where to start.

Ask for Money

By the time most students get around to thinking about applying for scholarships, they have already extolled their personal and academic virtues to such lengths in essays and interviews for college applications that even their own grandmothers wouldn't recognize them. The thought of filling out yet another application form fills students with dread. And why bother? Won't the same five or six kids who have been fighting over grade point averages since the fifth grade walk away with all the really good scholarships?

The truth is, most of the scholarships available to high school and college students are being offered because an organization wants to promote interest in a particular field, to encourage more students to become qualified to enter it, and to help those students afford an education. Certainly, having a good grade point average is a valuable asset, and many organizations granting scholarships request that only applicants with a minimum grade point average apply. More often than not, however, grade point averages aren't even mentioned; the focus is on the area of interest and what a student has done to distinguish himself or herself in that area. In fact, frequently the only requirement is that the scholarship applicant be studying a particular subject area.

❑ GUIDELINES

When applying for scholarships there are a few simple guidelines that can help ease the process considerably.

Plan Ahead

The absolute worst thing you can do is wait until the last minute. For one thing, obtaining recommendations or other supporting data in time to meet an application deadline is incredibly difficult. For another, no one does his or her best thinking or writing under the gun. So get off to a good start by reviewing scholarship applications as early as possible—months, even a year, in advance. If the current scholarship information isn't available, ask for a copy of last year's version. Once you have the scholarship information or application in hand, give it a thorough read. Try and determine how your experience or situation best fits into the scholarship, or even if it fits at all. Don't waste your time applying for a scholarship in turf management if you are interested in studying sports medicine.

If possible, research the award or scholarship, including past recipients and, where applicable, the person in whose name the scholarship is offered. If the scholarship was founded in honor a someone, try and get a feel for the spirit of that person's work. If you have any similar interests or experiences, don't hesitate to mention them.

Talk to others who received the scholarship, or to students currently studying in the same area or field of interest in which the scholarship is offered, and try to gain insight into possible applications or work related to that field. Doing this sort of research will mean that you have real answers when writing the essay that asks you why you want this scholarship— "I would benefit from receiving this scholarship because studying sports medicine will help me to assist athletes stay safe during competition and meet their athletic goals."

Take your time writing the essays. Make certain you are answering the question or questions on the application and not merely restating facts about yourself. Don't be afraid to get creative. Try and imagine what you would think of if you had to sift through hundreds of applications: What would you want to know about the candidate? What would convince you that someone was deserving of the scholarship? Work through several drafts and have someone whose advice you respect—a parent, teacher, or guidance counselor—review the essay for grammar and content.

Finally, if you know in advance which scholarships you want to apply for, there might still be time to stack the deck in your favor by getting an internship, volunteering, or working part time. Bottom line: The more you know about a scholarship and the sooner you learn it, the better.

Follow Directions

Think of it this way—many of the organizations that offer scholarships devote 99.9 percent of their time to something other than the scholarship for which you are applying. Don't make a nuisance of yourself by pestering them for information. Follow the directions you are given, even when asking for the application materials. If the scholarship information specifies that you write for information, write for it—and don't call.

Pay close attention to whether you're applying for an award, a scholarship, a prize, or financial aid. Often these words are used interchangeably, but just as often they have different meanings. An award is usually given for something you have done: built a park or helped distribute meals to the elderly; or something you have created: a design, an essay, a short film, a screenplay, or an invention. On the other hand, a scholarship is frequently a renewable sum of money that is given to a person to help defray the costs of college. Scholarships are given to candidates who meet the necessary criteria based on essays, eligibility, grades, or athletic ability, and sometimes all four.

Supply all the necessary documents, information, fees, etc., and make the deadlines. You won't win any scholarships by forgetting to include a recommendation from your health teacher or failing to postmark the application by the deadline. Bottom line: Get it right the first time, on time.

Apply Early

Once you have the application in hand, don't dawdle. If you've requested it far enough in advance, there shouldn't be any reason for you not to turn it well in advance of the deadline. You never know, if it comes down to two candidates, the deciding factor just might be your timeliness. Bottom line: Don't wait.

Be Yourself

Don't make promises you can't keep. There are plenty of hefty scholarships available, but if they all require you to study something that you don't enjoy, you'll be miserable in college. And the side effects from switching majors after you've accepted a scholarship could be even worse. Bottom line: Be yourself.

Don't Limit Yourself

There are many sources for scholarships, beginning with your guidance counselor and ending with the Internet. All of the search engines have education categories. Start there and search by keywords, such as "financial aid," "scholarship," "award." Don't be limited to the scholarships listed in these pages.

If you know of an organization related to or involved with the field of your choice, write a letter asking if they offer scholarships. If they don't offer scholarships, don't let that stop you. Write them another letter, or better yet, schedule a meeting with the president or someone in the public relations office and ask them if they would be willing to sponsor a scholarship for you. Of course, you'll need to prepare yourself well for such a meeting because you're selling a priceless commodity—yourself. Don't be shy, and be confident. Tell them all about yourself, what you want to study and why, and let them know what you would be willing to

do in exchange—volunteer at their favorite charity, write up reports on your progress in school, or work part time on school breaks and full time during the summer. Explain why you're a wise investment. Bottom line: The sky's the limit.

❏ THE LIST

American Alliance for Health, Physical Education, Recreation and Dance (AAHPERD)

Attn: Deb Callis
1900 Association Drive
Reston, VA 20191-1598
800-213-7193
dcallis@aahperd.org
http://www.aahperd.org/aahperd/
    template.cfm?template=presidents_
    scholarships.html

Applicants for the Ruth Abernathy Undergraduate Scholarship must be current members of AAHPERD (or join at time of application) who are majoring in the field of health, physical education, recreation, or dance. They must also be full-time students with a junior or senior status at a baccalaureate-granting college or university, maintain a 3.5 out of 4.0 GPA, demonstrate exceptional leadership abilities, and participate in community-service activities. Graduate students may also apply for this scholarship. Visit the alliance's Web site to download an application.

American Legion Baseball Scholarship

700 North Pennsylvania Street
Indianapolis, IN 46204-1129

ACY@legion.org
http://www.baseball.legion.org

The legion offers scholarships of $1,000. Applicants must be on the current roster of an American Legion baseball team, be high school graduates (or soon-to-be graduates), and demonstrate outstanding achievement in baseball. Applicants must be nominated by their American Legion team manager or head coach. Visit the American Legion's Web site to download an application and to find a list of addresses for each state's headquarters. Applicants should submit the application to their state's American Legion headquarters—and *not* to the national headquarters.

American Women in Radio and Television (AWRT)

8405 Greensboro Drive, Suite 800
McLean, VA 22102-5120
703-506-3290
info@awrt.org
http://www.awrt.org

Regional chapters of AWRT provide a variety of scholarships to college students interested in broadcasting. Applicants should visit AWRT's Web site to locate contact information for their local chapter.

Army ROTC

800-USA-ROTC
http://www.goarmy.com/rotc/
scholarships.jsp

Students planning to attend college or currently in college may apply for scholarships that pay tuition and some living expenses;

recipients must agree to accept a commission and serve in the Army on Active Duty or in a Reserve Component (U.S. Army Reserve or Army National Guard).

Association for Women in Sports Media

Attn: Rachel Cohen, Scholarship Coordinator
PO Box 11897
College Station, TX 77842-1897
AWSMintern@hotmail.com
http://www.awsmonline.org

Full-time undergraduate and graduate female students pursuing careers in sports-related writing, copyediting, public relations, broadcasting, Internet, or photography may apply for $1,000 Association for Women in Sports Media Scholarships and Internships. Visit the association's Web site for more information about internship options in various categories.

Association on American Indian Affairs

Scholarship Coordinator
966 Hungerford Drive, Suite 12-B
Rockville, MD 20850-1743
240-314-7155
general.aaia@verizon.net
http://www.indian-affairs.org

Undergraduate and graduate Native American students who are pursuing a variety of college majors can apply for scholarships ranging from $500 to $1,500. All applicants must provide proof of Native American heritage. Visit the association's Web site for more information.

Broadcast Education Association (BEA)
1771 N Street NW
Washington, DC 20036-2891
888-380-7222
beainfo@beaweb.org
http://www.beaweb.org

An association of university broadcasting faculty, industry professionals, and graduate students, BEA offers more than 10 annual scholarships (ranging from $1,250 to $5,000) in broadcasting for college students. Applicants must be able to demonstrate superior academic performance and a dedication to a career in broadcasting.

CollegeBoard.com
http://apps.collegeboard.com/
   cbsearch_ss/welcome.jsp

This testing service (PSAT, SAT, etc.) also offers a scholarship search engine at its Web site. It features scholarships (not all sports-related) worth nearly $3 billion. You can search by specific major (such as athletic training, sports/sports administration, and turf management) and a variety of other criteria.

CollegeNET
http://mach25.collegenet.com/cgi-
   bin/M25/index

CollegeNET features 600,000 scholarships (not all sports-related) worth more than $1.6 billion. You can search by keyword (such as "sports" or "athletics") or by creating a personality profile of your interests.

Columbia 300
Attn: Dale Garner
PO Box 13430
San Antonio, TX 78213-0430
http://columbia300.com/jjowdy.pdf

Graduating high school seniors who have been actively involved in the sport of bowling may apply for the $500 Columbia 300 John Jowdy Scholarship. Visit the organization's Web site to download an application.

Daughters of the American Revolution (DAR)
Attn: Scholarship Committee
1776 D Street NW
Washington, DC 20006-5303
202-628-1776
http://www.dar.org/natsociety/
   edout_scholar.cfm

General Scholarships are available to students who have been accepted to or who are currently enrolled in a college or university in the United States. Selection criteria include academic excellence, commitment to field of study, and financial need; applicants need not be affiliated with DAR. A scholarship program is also available for Native American students. Contact the Scholarship Committee for more information.

FastWeb
http://fastweb.monster.com

FastWeb is one of the best-known scholarship search engines around. It features 1.3 million scholarships (not all sports-related) worth more than $3 billion. To use this resource, you will need to register (free).

Golden Key International Honour Society

621 North Avenue NE, Suite C-100
Atlanta, GA 30308-2842
800-377-2401
http://www.goldenkey.org

Golden Key is an academic honor society that offers its members "opportunities for individual growth through leadership, career development, networking, and service." It awards more than $400,000 in scholarships annually through 18 different award programs. Membership in the society is selective; only the top 15 percent of college juniors and seniors—who may be pursuing education in any college major—are considered for membership by the organization. There is a one-time membership fee of $60 to $65. Contact the society for more information.

Golf Course Superintendents Association of America

Attn: Amanda Howard
1421 Research Park Drive
Lawrence, KS 66049-3858
800-472-7878
ahoward@gcsaa.org
http://www.gcsaa.org/students/
  scholarships/default.asp

Graduating high school seniors who are planning to study golf course management and who are accepted to accredited universities, colleges, or junior colleges for the next academic year may apply for the Scotts Company Scholars Program Scholarship. The primary goal of the program is to seek out promising students from diverse ethnic, cultural, and socioeconomic backgrounds. This includes females, minorities, and individuals with disabilities who wish to pursue careers in the greens industry. Scholarships are awarded in the amounts of $500 and $2,500. College freshmen, sophomores, or juniors may also apply for this program.

GuaranteedScholarships.com

http://www.guaranteed-scholarships.
  com

This Web site offers lists (by college) of scholarships, grants, and financial aid (not all sports-related) that "require no interview, essay, portfolio, audition, competition, or other secondary requirement."

Harness Horse Youth Foundation

16575 Carey Road
Westfield, IN 46074-8925
317-867-5877
hhyfetaylor@iquest.net
http://www.hhyf.org/scholarships.html

The foundation offers several scholarships to high school seniors and undergraduate students (preferably under age 25) with a background in harness horse racing. Applicants must be able to demonstrate both academic achievement and financial need. Visit the foundation's Web site to view eligibility requirements for each scholarship. Awards range from $500 to $3,000.

Hawaii Community Foundation

1164 Bishop Street, Suite 800
Honolulu, HI 96813-2817

scholarships@hcf-hawaii.org
http://www.
    hawaiicommunityfoundation.
    org/scholar/scholar.php

The foundation offers a variety of scholarships for high school seniors and college students planning to pursue or currently studying physical education, athletic training, kinesiology, exercise therapy, sports medicine, journalism, and communications while in college. Applicants must be residents of Hawaii and demonstrate financial need. Visit the foundation's Web site for more information and to apply online.

Hawaii High School Athletic Association

PO Box 62029
Honolulu, HI 96839-2029
808-587-4495
http://www.sportshigh.com/index.jsp

The association offers the Kaimana Award to high school graduating seniors who are attending a high school in Hawaii, who maintain at least a 3.0 GPA on a 4.0 scale, and play on at least one school athletic team. Lower-profile sports are given special consideration. Scholarships of up to $3,000 are awarded. Visit the association's Web site to download an application.

Health Occupations Students of America (HOSA)

6021 Morriss Road, Suite 111
    Flower Mound, TX 75028-3764
800-321-HOSA
http://www.hosa.org

HOSA works with schools "to promote career opportunities in the health care industry and to enhance the delivery of quality health care to all people." It teams with the following organizations to offer more than $40,000 in scholarships to students interested in health care careers: Delmar, Hobsons, Hospital Corporation of America, Kaiser Permanente Healthcare, National Honor Roll, National Technical Honor Society, Nursing Spectrum, and Who's Who Among American High School Students. Contact HOSA for more information.

Hispanic College Fund (HCF)

1717 Pennsylvania Avenue NW,
    Suite 460
Washington, DC 20006-4629
800-644-4223
hcf-info@hispanicfund.org
http://www.hispanicfund.org

The Hispanic College Fund, in collaboration with several major corporations, offers many scholarships for high school seniors and college students planning to attend or currently attending college. Applicants must be Hispanic, live in the United States or Puerto Rico, and have a GPA of at least 3.0 on a 4.0 scale. Contact the HCF for more information.

Idaho High School Activities Association (IHSAA)

PO Box 4667
Boise, ID 83711-4667
208-375-7027
admin@idhsaa.org
http://www.idhsaa.org/announce/
    home.asp

The association offers $1,000 Interscholastic Star Scholarships to Idaho high school juniors who demonstrate a commitment to sportsmanship and community/school involvement. Applicants must have participated in at least one athletic IHSAA activity and one nonathletic IHSAA activity. Nonathletic activities include cheerleading, dance/drill, drama, speech, debate, vocal music, and instrumental music. Visit the association's Web site to download an application.

Illinois Career Resource Network
http://www.ilworkinfo.com/icrn.htm

Created by the Illinois Department of Employment Security, this useful site offers a great scholarship search engine, as well as detailed information on careers (including those in athletics). You can search for sports-related scholarships based on majors (such as athletic training, exercise science and kinesiotherapy, and sports and fitness management), and other criteria. This site is available to everyone, not just Illinois residents; you can get a password by simply visiting the site. The Illinois Career Information System is just one example of sites created by state departments of employment security (or departments of labor) to assist students with financial and career-related issues. After checking out this site, visit your state's department of labor Web site to see what it offers.

Louisiana High School Athletic Association
8075 Jefferson Highway
Baton Rouge, LA 70809-7675
225-925-0100
http://www.lhsaa.org/Scholarships.htm

The association offers several scholarships to Louisiana students who are involved in some aspect of high school athletics. Applicants must be high school students who intend to pursue postsecondary education. Interested candidates should visit the association's Web site to learn more about eligibility requirements for specific scholarships. Scholarships range from $500 to $1,000.

Marine Corps Scholarship Foundation
PO Box 3008
Princeton, NJ 08543-3008
800-292-7777
mcsfnj@mcsf.org
http://www.mcsf.org/site/
    c.ivKVLaMTIuG/b.1677655/k.BEA8/
    Home.htm

The foundation helps children of marines and former marines with scholarships of up to $5,000 for postsecondary study. To be eligible, you must be a high school graduate or registered as an undergraduate student at an accredited college or vocational/technical institute. Additionally, your total family gross income may not exceed $63,000. Contact the foundation for further details.

Michigan High School Athletic Association
1661 Ramblewood Drive
East Lansing, MI 48823-7392
517-332-5046
afrushour@mhsaa.com
http://www.mhsaa.com/recognition/
    sahome.htm

The association offers $1,000 scholarships to Michigan high school seniors who are enrolled in a Michigan High School Athletic Association member school, are participating in at least one sport, and have achieved a varsity letter in a sport prior to their senior year. Applicants must also demonstrate academic achievement by maintaining a 3.5 GPA on a 4.0 scale. Visit the association's Web site to view a complete list of eligible sports and eligibility requirements.

National Collegiate Athletic Association (NCAA)

700 West Washington Street
PO Box 6222
Indianapolis, IN 46206-6222
317-917-6222
http://www.ncaa.org/wps/portal

High school seniors who intend to participate in athletics at the collegiate level in a Division I, II, or III school may apply for Undergraduate Athletic Scholarships. Applicants should visit the NCAA's Web site to view links to their schools of choice and eligibility requirements for different schools and sports. Division I and II athletic scholarships are offered *only* through individual schools, and *not* the NCAA. Contact your school of choice for specific eligibility requirements. Division III schools only award scholarships for academics, and not athletics. Visit the NCAA's Web site for links to contacts at individual schools. You must contact your school directly for information about athletic scholarships and tryouts. Scholarships are also available to undergraduate students.

Navy: Education: Earn Money For College

http://www.navy.com/education/earnmoneyforcollege

The U.S. Navy offers several funding programs for college study. Students who receive money to attend college are typically required to serve a specific number of years in the navy after graduation. Other students take advantage of programs that allow them to join the navy and complete their degrees during their service obligation. Contact your local recruiter or visit the navy's Web site for details.

New Mexico Higher Education Department

1068 Cerrillos Road
Santa Fe, NM 87505-1650
800-279-9777
ofelia.morales@state.nm.us
http://hed.state.nm.us

Students enrolled or planning to enroll in a public New Mexico college or university and participate in a sport while in attendance may apply for athletic scholarships. Applicants do not need to be residents of New Mexico. Applicants should contact the appropriate athletic department or the financial aid office of any public New Mexico college or university for information on the application, recruitment, and the tryout process.

North Carolina High School Athletic Association

Attn: Karen DeHart
PO Box 3216
Chapel Hill, NC 27515-3216

919-962-0293
http://www.nchsaa.org/genPage/
    index.pl?pgid=463

Graduating high school seniors in North Carolina who will enroll as full-time undergraduates in a U.S. college or university for the fall semester following high school graduation may apply for the Clary Medal Award. Applicants must have participated in at least two sports during high school, maintained a 3.2 GPA on a 4.0 scale, and participated in nonathletic extracurricular activities. They also must demonstrate a commitment to service through volunteer work and community service. Visit the association's Web site for more information.

Patrick Kerr Skateboard Scholarship
PO Box 2054
Jenkintown, PA 19046-0654
info@skateboardscholarship.org
http://www.skateboardscholarship.
    org/index.html

Graduating high school seniors who possess at least a 2.5 GPA on a 4.0 scale, are U.S. citizens, and are planning to enroll in a two- or four-year undergraduate program in the fall may apply for the Patrick Kerr Skateboard Scholarship. Applicants must be passionate skateboarders. One winner receives $5,000, and three winners receive $1,000. Visit the organization's Web site for additional information.

Professional Grounds Management Society
720 Light Street
Baltimore, MD 21230-3850

800-609-PGMS
pgms@assnhqtrs.com
http://www.pgms.org/
    seamanscholarship.htm

High school seniors and college-age students planning to pursue or currently pursuing a degree in landscape and grounds management, turf management, irrigation technology, or a closely related field may apply for the Anne Seaman Memorial Scholarship. Visit the society's Web site to download an application.

Radio-Television News Directors Foundation
RTNDF Scholarships
Attn: Irving Washington
1600 K Street NW, Suite 700
Washington, DC 20006-2806
202-467-5218
irvingw@rtndf.org
http://www.rtnda.org/asfi/index.asp

The foundation offers a variety of scholarships to college students.

Applicants for the $6,000 George Foreman Tribute to Lyndon B. Johnson Scholarship must be enrolled full-time sophomores, juniors, or seniors at the University of Texas–Austin and interested in pursuing a career in electronic journalism.

Applicants for the $1,000 Lou and Carole Prato Sports Reporting Scholarship must be full-time college sophomores, juniors, or seniors who are studying radio or television sports reporting.

Applicants for the $2,500 Presidents' Scholarship must be enrolled full-time college sophomores, juniors, or seniors who are studying radio and television news.

Applicants for the $1,000 Mike Reynolds Journalism Scholarship must be enrolled full-time college sophomores, juniors, or seniors who have good writing ability, excellent grades, a dedication to the news business, a strong interest in pursuing a career in electronic journalism, and a demonstrated need for financial assistance.

The foundation also offers several scholarships for minorities. Minority students whose career objective is electronic journalism (radio or television), and have at least one full year of college remaining, may apply for the Carole Simpson Scholarship ($2,000), the Ed Bradley Scholarship ($10,000), and the Ken Kashiwahara Scholarship ($2,500). Applicants must attend college full time. High school seniors may also apply for these scholarships.

Sallie Mae

http://www.collegeanswer.com/
  paying/scholarship_search/pay_
  scholarship_search.jsp

This Web site offers a scholarship database of more than 2.4 million awards (not all sports-related) worth more than $15 billion. You must register (free) to use the database.

Salute to Education

2600 Douglas Road, Suite 610
Coral Gables, FL 33134-6100
305-476-7709
steinfo@stescholarships.org
http://www.stescholarships.org/SC_
  categories.html

Graduating high school seniors who attend a Miami-Dade or Broward County, Florida, high school and who also reside in one of these counties may apply for $1,000 Salute to Education Athletics Scholarships. They also must be legal residents of the United States, have a minimum weighted GPA of 3.0, demonstrate a commitment to service by participating in at least one school or community organization, and intend to pursue a college degree at an accredited institution after graduation. Applicants must have participated in varsity athletics for at least two years, while demonstrating good leadership skills, a positive attitude, and good sportsmanship. Visit the organization's Web site for more information.

Scholar Athlete Milk Mustache of the Year Scholarships (SAMMY)

c/o Infoscan
Attn: SAMMY
6701 Democracy Boulevard,
  Suite 300
Bethesda, MD 20817-7500
http://www.whymilk.com/win_
  sammy.htm

High school graduating seniors who participate in a sport and who also demonstrate academic excellence and a commitment to community service may apply for $7,500 SAMMY Awards. Applicants must intend to enter an accredited undergraduate program in the fall following graduation from high school. This scholarship is sponsored by the Got Milk? Campaign, and winners agree to participate in a national milk mustache advertisement. Visit the organization's Web site to apply.

Scholarship America
4960 Viking Drive, Suite 110
Edina, MN 55435-5314
800-279-2083
http://www.scholarshipamerica.org

This organization works through its local Dollars for Scholars chapters throughout the United States. In 2005, it awarded more than $29 million in scholarships to students. Visit Scholarship America's Web site for more information.

Scholarships.com
http://www.scholarships.com

Scholarships.com offers a free college scholarship search engine (although you must register to use it) and financial aid information. Its awards database features 3,000 listings worth up to $3 billion in aid.

Scripps Howard Foundation
PO Box 5380
312 Walnut Street
Cincinnati, OH 45202-5378
513-977-3030
http://foundation.scripps.com/
foundation/programs/scholarships/
scholarships.html

The foundation offers scholarships to undergraduate and graduate students who are interested in journalism or graphic arts (as applied to the newspaper industry). Contact the foundation for eligibility requirements and participating schools.

SportsToSchool.com Scholarship
PO Box 6071
Middletown, RI 02842-0900
401-849-2639
info@sportstoschool.com
http://www.sportstoschool.com/
scholarship.html

High school students who participate in a high school sport and who want to continue to play that sport in college may apply for $1,000 SportsToSchool.com College Scholarships. Each applicant should submit an online essay that includes contact information and a short paragraph about how sports have played a positive role in his or her life. Visit the organization's Web site to apply online.

United Negro College Fund (UNCF)
http://www.uncf.org/scholarships/
index.asp

Visitors to the UNCF's Web site can search for thousands of scholarships and grants, many of which are administered by the UNCF. High school seniors and undergraduate and graduate students are eligible. The search engine allows you to search by major (such as business, communications, health, journalism, management, marketing, medicine, statistics, and television production), state, scholarship title, grade level, and achievement score.

United States Bowling Congress
5301 South 76th Street
Greendale, WI 53129-1128
800-514-2695
http://www.bowl.com/scholarships/
main.aspx

Visit this organization's Web site for links to more than $6 million in scholarship money that is offered by bowling associations and councils, certified tournaments, and proprietors throughout the United States.

Women's Western Golf Foundation

802 West Country Meadows
Peoria, IL 61614-2057
cocomc2000@comcast.net
http://www.wwga.org/scholarship_info.htm

Female high school seniors who are U.S. citizens, meet college entrance requirements, and plan to enroll at an accredited college or university may apply for $2,000 Undergraduate Scholarships. Applicants must have completed and submitted the Free Application for Federal Student Aid, demonstrate financial need, and maintain a minimum 3.0 GPA on a scale of 4.0. Contact the foundation for details.

Look to the Pros

The following professional organizations offer a variety of materials, from career brochures to lists of accredited schools to salary surveys. Many of them also publish journals and newsletters that you should become familiar with. Many also have annual conferences that you might be able to attend. (While you may not be able to attend a conference as a participant, it may be possible to "cover" one for your school or even your local paper, especially if your school has a related club.)

When contacting professional organizations, keep in mind that they all exist primarily to serve their members, be it through continuing education, professional licensure, political lobbying, or just "keeping up with the profession." While many are strongly interested in promoting their profession and passing information about it to the general public, these busy professional organizations do not exist solely to provide you with information. Whether you call or write, be courteous, brief, and to the point. Know what you need and ask for it. If the organization has a Web site, check it out first: what you're looking for may be available there for downloading, or you may find a list of prices or instructions. Finally, be aware that organizations, like people, move. To save time when writing, first confirm the address, preferably with a quick phone call to the organization itself, "Hello, I'm calling to confirm your address . . . ."

❏ THE SOURCES

Accrediting Council on Education in Journalism and Mass Communications

University of Kansas School of Journalism and Mass Communications
Stauffer-Flint Hall, 1435 Jayhawk Boulevard
Lawrence, KS 66045-7575
785-864-3973
http://www2.ku.edu/~acejmc/STUDENT/PROGLIST.SHTML

Visit the council's Web site for a list of accredited programs in journalism and mass communications.

Amateur Athletic Union (AAU)

PO Box 22409
Lake Buena Vista, FL 32830-2409
407-934-7200
http://www.aausports.org

Contact the AAU for information on participating in sports of all types and its various programs around the country, including the AAU Junior Olympics and the President's Challenge National Youth Physical Fitness Program.

American Alliance for Health, Physical Education, Recreation and Dance (AAHPERD)

1900 Association Drive
Reston, VA 20191-1502
800-213-7193
info@aahperd.org
http://www.aahperd.org

AAHPERD is an umbrella organization for several sports associations. Visit its Web site for more information.

American Baseball Coaches Association

108 South University Avenue, Suite 3
Mount Pleasant, MI 48858-2327
989-775-3300
abca@abca.org
http://www.abca.org

Visit the association's Web site for links to polls/scores and useful articles on coaching baseball.

American College of Sports Medicine (ACSM)

PO Box 1440
Indianapolis, IN 46206-1440
317-637-9200
http://www.acsm.org

The college offers information on health and fitness and becoming a board-certified athletic trainer. A variety of useful free publications are available at the college's Web site, including *Careers in Sports Medicine and Exercise Science*. Also available for a low cost via mail is *What Is an Exercise Physiologist?* which defines exercise physiology, the duties and responsibilities, work environments, and educational requirements. The ACSM also offers Graduate and Undergraduate Programs Link, an online directory of postsecondary programs in sports medicine and exercise science.

American Orthopaedic Society for Sports Medicine

6300 North River Road, Suite 500
Rosemont, IL 60018-4235
847-292-4900
http://www.sportsmed.org

The society's comprehensive Web site offers a fun and interesting way to learn about what's new in sports medicine. It includes an Ask the Sports Doctor section that covers various sports medicine topics.

American Sportscasters Association

225 Broadway, Suite 2030
New York, NY 10007-3742
212-227-8080
http://www.
    americansportscastersonline.com

Visit the association's Web site to read articles and interviews about sportscasting and to learn more about membership for college students.

American Sports Medicine Institute

2660 10th Avenue South, Suite 505
Birmingham, AL 35205-1626
205-918-0000
http://www.asmi.org

The institute offers information on fellowships, a research program for college students, useful publications, and the field of sports medicine at its Web site.

American Statistical Association

1429 Duke Street
Alexandria, VA 22314-3415
888-231-3473
asainfo@amstat.org
http://www.amstat.org

Contact the association for information on careers in statistics and schools that offer degrees in statistics.

Associated Press Sports Editors

c/o The Dallas Morning News:
    Sports Day
508 Young Street
Dallas, TX 75202-4808
214-977-8222
http://apse.dallasnews.com

Associated Press Sports Editors is a membership organization that strives to improve print journalistic standards in sports newsrooms. Web site visitors will find up-to-date news articles regarding industry happenings, a job board, and a downloadable monthly newsletter, as well as links to Web sites for all major professional sports organizations and leagues. Membership information, including an in-depth profile of the organization, is also included.

Association for Education in Journalism and Mass Communication

234 Outlet Pointe Boulevard
Columbia, SC 29210-5667
803-798-0271
http://www.aejmc.org

This organization provides general educational information on all areas of journalism, including newspapers, magazines, television, and radio.

Association for Women in Sports Media (AWSM)

PO Box 11897
College Station, TX 77842-1897
http://www.awsmonline.org

The AWSM is a membership organization of women and men employed in sports-related writing, editing, broadcast and production, public relations, and communications. Visit its Web site for information on internships and scholarships.

Association of Minor League Umpires

http://www.amlu.org

Visit the association's Web site for information on careers in baseball umpiring and to participate in an online forum.

Broadcast Education Association (BEA)

1771 N Street NW
Washington, DC 20036-2891
888-380-7222
beainfo@beaweb.org
http://www.beaweb.org

An association of university broadcasting faculty, industry professionals, and graduate students, BEA offers annual scholarships in broadcasting for college juniors, seniors, and graduate students. Visit its Web site for useful information about broadcast education and the broadcasting industry.

Golf Course Superintendents Association of America (GCSAA)

1421 Research Park Drive
Lawrence, KS 66049-3859
800-472-7878
infobox@gcsaa.org
http://www.gcsaa.org

For comprehensive information on golf course management careers, internships, job listings, turfgrass management programs, membership for college students, and certification, contact the GCSAA.

International Association of Approved Basketball Officials (IAABO)

12321 Middlebrook Road
Germantown, MD 20875-1300
301-540-5180
http://www.iaabo.org

Contact the IAABO for information on training schools and becoming a basketball official.

Ladies Professional Golf Association (LPGA)

100 International Golf Drive
Daytona Beach, FL 32124-1092
386-274-6200
http://www.lpga.com/default_rr.aspx

The LPGA is the longest running women's sports association in the world. Visit its Web site for information on tour professionals, internships, and youth programs.

Major League Baseball (MLB)

75 Ninth Avenue, 5th Floor
New York, NY 10011-7006
866-800-1275
http://mlb.com

Visit the MLB Web site for information on professional baseball, fantasy camps, and statistics. An online fan forum is also available.

Major League Soccer

http://www.mlsnet.com/MLS/index.jsp

Major League Soccer is the professional league for male soccer players. It has 12 teams. Visit its Web site for information on players, teams, standings, transactions, and youth camps and competitions.

Minor League Baseball

http://www.minorleaguebaseball.com

This organization oversees minor league baseball. To learn how to become a minor league umpire, visit http://www.minorleaguebaseball.com/app/milb/info/umpires.jsp?mc=_ump_career.

National Association for Girls and Women in Sport

c/o American Alliance for Health, Physical Education, Recreation & Dance
1900 Association Drive, PO Box 385
Reston, VA 20191-1598
800-321-0789
http://www.aahperd.org/nagws/template.cfm

Contact the association for information on membership for college students, scholarships for college students, and opportunities for women in sports.

National Association for Sport and Physical Education

1900 Association Drive
Reston, VA 20191-1598
703-476-3400
http://www.aahperd.org/naspe/
template.cfm?template=main.html

Contact the association for information on membership for college students, useful publications, and internships.

National Association of Broadcasters

1771 N Street NW
Washington, DC 20036-2891
202-429-5300
nab@nab.org
http://www.nab.org

The association provides information on broadcast education, scholarships, and useful publications at its Web site.

National Association of Sports Officials (NASO)

2017 Lathrop Avenue
Racine, WI 53405-3758
262-632-5448
naso@naso.org
http://www.naso.org

Contact the NASO for information on sports officials' camps and clinics and becoming a sports official. The association also publishes *Referee* magazine.

National Athletic Trainers' Association (NATA)

2952 Stemmons Freeway
Dallas, TX 75247-6113
214-637-6282
http://www.nata.org

For information on the career of athletic trainer, educational requirements, certification, membership for college students, and useful publications, visit the association's Web site.

National Basketball Association (NBA)

http://www.nba.com

Visit the NBA's Web site for information on member teams, statistics, and fantasy leagues.

National Collegiate Athletic Association (NCAA)

700 West Washington Street,
PO Box 6222
Indianapolis, IN 46206-6222
317-917-6222
http://www.ncaa.org

The NCAA is by far the largest athletic collegiate association with member schools throughout the United States. It sets up recruiting guidelines and schedules, and it also stipulates the number and amount of scholarships that each school may offer to student athletes. Visit its Web site for information on eligibility, sports, statistics, scholarships, and useful publications, such as the *NCAA Guide for the College-Bound Student-Athlete* and *Career in Professional Athletics*.

National Football League (NFL)

http://www.nfl.com

Visit the NFL's Web site for scores, statistics, a free newsletter, youth football programs, and links to member teams.

National High School Athletic Coaches Association (NHSACA)
office@hscoaches.org
http://www.hscoaches.org

Contact the association for information on high school coaching opportunities.

National Hockey League (NHL)
http://www.nhl.com

Visit the NHL's Web site for information on teams, statistics, scores, a free e-mail newsletter, and tips on playing and coaching hockey.

National Pro Fastpitch
4610 South Ulster Drive, Suite 150
Denver, CO 80237-4326
303-290-7494
http://www.profastpitch.com

National Pro Fastpitch is a professional league of fastpitch women's softball players. It has teams in seven cities in the United States. Visit its Web site for information on teams and players, a message board, and facts on women in sports.

National Soccer Coaches Association of America
6700 Squibb Road, Suite 215
Mission, KS 66202-3252
800-458-0678
info@nscaa.com
http://www.nscaa.com

Visit the association's Web site for useful articles on coaching.

North American Society for Sport Management
http://www.nassm.com

Visit the society's Web site for information on membership for college students and a list of colleges and universities that offer sports management programs.

Professional Bowlers Association (PBA)
719 Second Avenue, Suite 701
Seattle, WA 98104-1747
206-332-9688
http://www.pba.com

Visit the PBA's Web site for information on professional bowling, the Billy Welu Scholarship, and a primer on bowling.

Professional Golfers' Association of America (PGA)
100 Avenue of the Champions
Palm Beach, Florida 33418
561-624-8400
http://www.pga.com

Contact the PGA for information on professional golf, tournaments, and membership.

Professional Grounds Management Society
720 Light Street
Baltimore, MD 21230-3850
800-609-7467
pgms@assnhqtrs.com
http://www.pgms.org

For information on membership for college students, the Anne Seaman Memorial Scholarship, and certification, visit the society's Web site.

Sporting Goods Manufacturers Association (SGMA)
1150 17th Street NW, Suite 850
Washington DC 20036-4616

202-775-1762
info@sgma.com
http://www.sgma.com

Visit the SGMA's Web site for information on the sports manufacturing industry.

Sports Turf Managers Association

805 New Hampshire Street, Suite E
Lawrence, KS 66044-2774
800-323-3875
stmahq@st.omhcoxmail.com
http://www.sportsturfmanager.org

For information on scholarships for college students, links to colleges and universities that offer training in sports turf management, and certification, visit the association's Web site.

United States Association for Blind Athletes

33 North Institute Street
Colorado Springs, CO 80903-3508
719-630-0422
http://www.usaba.org

The association seeks to help blind or visually impaired athletes in the United States to reach their athletic goals. Visit its Web site for information on sporting events, sports adaptations, sports camps, and junior membership.

United States Figure Skating Association

20 First Street
Colorado Springs, CO 80906-3624
719-635-5200
info@usfigureskating.org
http://www.usfsa.org

Visit the association's Web site for information on competitive figure skating and training programs.

United States Tennis Association (USTA)

http://www.usta.com

Visit the USTA's Web site for information on tennis circuits, junior and professional tournaments and schedules, and other details about the sport.

Women's National Basketball Association (WNBA)

Olympic Tower, 645 Fifth Avenue
New York, NY 10022-5910
212-688-9622
http://www.wnba.com

This professional league for female professional basketball players has 14 teams throughout the United States. The WNBA Web site offers information on players, teams, and transactions, as well as a glossary of basketball-related terms.

Women's Sports Foundation

Eisenhower Park
East Meadow, NY 11554
800-227-3988
info@womenssportsfoundation.org
http://www.womenssportsfoundation.
  org

This organization seeks to increase opportunities for girls and women in sports. Visit its Web site for an overview of careers in sports, useful articles, and a searchable database of postsecondary sports business and administration educational programs. A free online newsletter is also available.

World Umpires Association
PO Box 394
Neenah, WI 54957-0394
http://www.worldumpires.com

Visit the association's Web site for information on union representation for Major League Baseball umpires, training opportunities, and interesting facts about umpires.

Index

Entries and page numbers in **bold** indicate major treatment of a topic.